RainMaker

Strategic Partnering with Attorneys and Accountants
to Create a Pipeline of New Affluent Clients

by Russ Alan Prince and Brett Van Bortel

ISBN: 0-87218-687-3

This publication is designed to provide accurate and authoritative information in regard to the subject matter covered. It is sold with the understanding that the publisher is not engaged in rendering legal, accounting or other professional service. If legal advice or other expert assistance is required, the services of a competent professional should be sought. — **From a Declaration of Principles jointly adopted by a Committee of the American Bar Association and a Committee of Publishers and Associations.**

Printed in U.S.A.

Dedication

To Sandi,
Who keeps me running
Russ Alan Prince

To Victoria, My Parents and Nicholas,
My love for you all stands outside of time.
Brett Van Bortel

About the Authors

Russ Alan Prince

Russ Alan Prince is President of the market research and consulting firm Prince & Associates Inc. and a leading authority on the private wealth industry. Mr. Prince consults to high-net-worth families on accessing various family office and wealth management services. He also works with financial and legal experts who provide cutting-edge strategies and concepts to families with exceptional wealth. Mr. Prince is a columnist with various publications and is the author of 33 previous books.

Brett Van Bortel

Brett Van Bortel is Director of Consulting Services with VK Consulting, the largest group of its kind in the industry, dedicated to helping financial advisors build, improve, and expand their business. While Mr. Van Bortel has built numerous programs, his dominant focus is on the affluent market, utilizing research insights to develop programs effective at the field level on Wealth Management, Client Advocacy/Referral Systems, and the subject of this book – garnering high-net-worth referrals from non-competing professionals. Mr. Van Bortel also provides extensive individualized and group coaching services to financial advisors on these subjects.

Books authored and co-authored by Russ Alan Prince and/or Brett Van Bortel

1. *Wealth Preservation for Physicians: Advanced Planning Strategies for Affluent Doctors* (Wealth Management Press, 2006).

2. *Cultivating the Middle-Class Millionaire: How Financial Advisors are Failing Their Wealthy Clients and What They Can Do About It* (Wealth Management Press, 2005).

3. *Selecting a Coach: Seven Guidelines for Financial Advisors* (CFPN, 2005).

4. *Inside the Family Office: Managing the Fortunes of the Exceptionally Wealthy* (Wealth Management Press, 2004).

5. *Safe & Sound: A Proven Methodology for Protecting the Wealthy* (National Underwriter, 2004).

6. *Women of Wealth: Understanding Today's Affluent Female Investor* (National Underwriter, 2004).

7. *The Private Client Lawyer: Now and in the Future* (Wealth Management Press, 2003).

8. *Creating a Pipeline of New Affluent Clients: Building Strategic Partnerships with Lawyers & Accountants* (National Underwriter, 2003).

9. *Wealth Management: The New Business Model for Financial Advisors* (Wealth Management Press, 2003).

10. *Accountants as Wealth Managers: The New Paradigm for Providing Financial Services* (Institutional Investor, 2003).

11. *Advanced Planning with the Ultra-Affluent: A Framework for Professional Advisors* (Institutional Investor, 2002).

12. *Giving Wisely: Maximizing Your Charitable Giving* (Giving Capital, 2002).

13. *The World of Registered Representatives: Insights and Opportunities for Brokerage and Investment Management Firms* (Institutional Investor, 2002).

14. *The Millionaire's Advisor: High-Touch, High-Profit Relationship Management Strategies of Advisors to the Wealthy* (Institutional Investor, 2002).

15. *eWealth: Understanding the Internet Millionaire* (Institutional Investor, 2001).

16. *Marketing Mutual Funds Through Independent Advisors* (Institutional Investor, 2001).

17. *Value-Added Wholesaling: The New Paradigm for Marketing Financial Products Through Advisors* (Institutional Investor, 2000).

18. *Advisor 2000: Strategies for Success in the New Millennium* (High-Net-Worth Press, 2000).

19. *High-Net-Worth Psychology: Finding, Winning and Keeping Affluent Investors* (High-Net-Worth Press, 1999).

20. *Winning the War for the Wealthy: How Life Insurance Companies can Dominate the Upscale Markets* (High-Net-Worth Press, 1999).

21. *Private Wealth: Insights in the High-Net-Worth Market* (Institutional Investor, 1999).

Foreword

The financial advisory business is at its core a business of finding and developing lasting relationships with clients. A goal that is at once simple and confoundingly complex. For this reason, I want to introduce the RainMaker process as a proven way to achieve this noble goal with a quick story that demonstrates the enormous leverage, likely problems, and potential profitability of finding just one good attorney or accountant to build a partnership with.

This is a story about a successful independent advisor named Gary from a major city in Ohio. Gary is very successful by any measure. His income is in the high six figure range, that's income not production. However, he wanted more and realized that if he continued the same activities he'd been doing the last 18 years, he'd end up with the same output. It's why people talk about plateauing so much in our industry. Accordingly, Gary committed himself to opening up a new revenue stream of affluent referrals through Attorneys and Accountants.

Gary initiated several strategies concurrently to find any attorney or accountant that could make a career changing referral. Eventually, he got a referral to one T&E Attorney through one of his wealthier clients. Prior to this meeting, Gary had been coached to make the conversation about the Attorney, his business, his clientele, his goals, his problems, his successes, and even failures. And not to sell himself, "Let me show you my money management process…"

Gary began the meeting by trying to build a little personal rapport, and then quickly moved the conversation to the Attorney's business, specifically asking what problems the attorney's clients were bringing him. With that, the attorney described one client who'd put a call into him two weeks ago. He was a small business owner, complaining that his retirement plan was top-heavy. Gary listened closely and suggested a viable solution to deal with the problem. The attorney told Gary he "loved" the idea. Not liked it, not thought it was interesting, but "loved" it. Gary walked out of the meeting thinking this is easier than I thought. It immediately got harder. Two months went by without a phone call or email from that attorney.

Gary realized that this trail was going to grow completely cold unless he got proactive on it. Gary met the Attorney a second time and got the same result – vague, lofty promises and no action. A few months later, Gary tried yet a third time and invited the Attorney out to play golf. While playing golf, the attorney brings up a third client whom is a high level executive in a publicly traded company with a sizeable concentrated stock position. The client is eager, if not anxious, to diversify. Gary again listened to the problem and again kicks out a few ideas.

Finally, six months into this process, this is where the story takes a turn for Gary's betterment. This time instead of saying he'd call him later, the attorney told Gary that when they got to the 19th hole, that he wanted to go to their cars, grab their calendars, and find several dates to offer to his client. Then he wanted to sit down with Gary and strategize on how to present this idea "to his client."

Gary said later he wasn't sure what accounted for the change. He wasn't sure if it was just right place, right time. But it later dawned on him, that during those first two meetings, which Gary had presumed were a complete waste of time, he had actually built up the trust, relationship, and confidence this attorney needed before he was willing to take Gary and put him in front of one of his best clients. Long story short, Gary walked into that meeting and walked out with an $8 million client. Since this time, he has become that attorney's right hand man for any financially related questions his clients have, and he has also gotten another client that literally dwarfs this client in value.

However, the core point of this story is this. If you want the most, the biggest, and the wealthiest referrals possible, you need to partner with the people that already have them as clients, but need the products and services you can provide. What Prince and Van Bortel have done in this book is literally peal back the curtain and look at the process used by the most successful advisors in the industry to build partnerships with attorneys and accountants, creating a pipeline of wealthy client referrals.

~ Scott West
Managing Director
Van Kampen Investments
January 2006

Table of Contents

Believe those who are seeking the truth. Doubt those who find it.

~ Andre Gide

Chapter 1

The *Secret* to Sourcing New Affluent Clients

"Inches make champions"

– Vince Lombardi

To be exceptionally successful it is valuable to critically examine the methods and processes employed by the most successful financial advisors in the country. And by "successful," we are focusing on personal income (after all expenses but before personal taxes). In considering the "best of the best," we find that there are 1,200 financial advisors – across all distribution channels – who consistently (each year for at least three years) pocket a minimum of $1 million per year.

The Critical Traits of the Elite 1200

Adam is a member of a very small "club" of financial advisors. He's one of the Elite 1200. Adam isn't really smarter than many of his peers. Nor has his investment performance for his clients been superior to most of his peers. Nevertheless, Adam pocketed over $2 million a year, for the last six years.

Compared to most other financial advisors, Adam is strongly interested in being financially successful. In fact, he doesn't compare himself to other financial advisors. They are not his baseline. Instead, he is looking upwards at his very affluent clients. It's no secret Adam wants to make money and his wealthy clients understand and appreciate this. They know that his commitment to become very wealthy translates into a commitment to deliver exceptional service to them.

Adam has a mere 92 clients, 17 of which he considers his core clients. Products and services for these core clients result in nearly 75% of Adam's income. Because of the critical importance of these core clients to Adam's ongoing success, he knows them inside and out. He knows their perceptions and wishes for their families. He knows their dreams and fears. He even knows all about their pets. It's pretty much impossible to have such a deep understanding about all his clients, but when it comes to his core clients, Adam knows them as well as he knows his own family and dear friends.

Like other members of the Elite 1200, Adam can recognize where his expertise can benefit his clients, as well as prospects, in real time. That is, as Adam learns about issues and concerns that impact his clients, he's able to see where he can benefit them. This doesn't mean Adam is a financial services polymath, able to do everything for them. On the contrary, Adam's specialty is money management, yet he's able to recognize fact patterns and is positioned and connected to bring in the appropriate experts.

Another trait contributing to Adam's success is that he invests in his business. This includes taking a long-term approach because he clearly recognizes the time frames involved in working with significant private wealth.

Now, if you look across the financial advisory universe as we have, you'll see quite a number of advisors who – save for them being less successful with larger client bases – have the same characteristics as Adam, save one. Adam is able to consistently access very wealthy clients. He's a rainmaker. And, he makes rain by creating strategic partnerships with attorneys.

All in all, there are 1,200 financial advisors who are in the same "class" as Adam. We refer to these financial advisors as the Elite 1200. Moreover, the Elite 1200 share six critical traits:

- *They're strongly financially motivated with excellent work habits.* Despite their substantial incomes, they're motivated to improve. This entails both working hard and smart. The phrase, "The good is the enemy of the great" is applicable. Their ambition is not softened by their success.

- *They have a deep understanding of their core clients.* They know their core clients exceptionally well, literally the same way many of us know our best friends. They stay current with the changing situations of these clients, and are cognizant of the impact any changes might have on the financial and personal situations of these core clients. A process that has been proven to be especially powerful in profiling clients that is employed by the Elite 1200 in one form or another is the Whole Client Model, a mechanism to uncover needs and provide wealth management services (see *Chapter 11, Filling the Pipeline*).

- *They can identify opportunities for financial products and services in real time.* They can address, in the moment, concerns and issues, knowing the role various financial products and services can play. This is not to say they're polymaths when it comes to the financial services universe, just that they're able to spot possibilities.

- *They can source the products and services needed by the affluent.* The ability to access and deliver on the financial needs and wants of the wealthy is essential in order to be successful. They are more often Wealth Managers, not just Investment Managers.

- *They take a long-term approach to their practices.* As opposed to short-term hits, the Elite 1200 are seeking to build very successful practices and they recognize this takes time. Though the wealthy may make their decisions at a glacial pace, they impact the financial advisor's bottom line with equal power. The Elite 1200 understand that the incubation period to convert a wealthy prospect into a client can take many months or, in some cases, years. They are looking to the future and understand what it takes to be effective.

- *They're highly adept at garnering new affluent client referrals.* To make $1 million a year, year after year, requires being able to garner wealthy clients. While some advisors can reach this level of success by focusing on institutional business, for the overwhelming majority of the Elite 1200, the money is with the monied class.

In coaching financial advisors for many years, we've found that these six critical traits are pervasive among nearly all of them. The real issues are the levels of these critical traits among financial advisors.

Take a moment to consider:

- Do you want to make more money? A lot more money? Are you willing to work – work hard *and* smart – to become personally wealthy?

- Do you have a deep understanding of your core clients? If not, are you willing to make an effort to learn how to develop such an understanding?

- Can you identify opportunities for financial products and services in real time? If not, are you willing to take the time and make the effort to learn?

- Can you source a broad array of financial products and services? If not, are you willing to put the appropriate network in place to do so?

- Are you willing to work at your practice? Are you willing to take a long-term view?

- Are you currently garnering as many new affluent clients as you would like? Are you willing to learn how?

In the end, the Elite 1200 are not sages with access to the "sacred wisdom." Nor are the Elite 1200 so much superior to the rest of the financial advisory universe. On the contrary, everything that makes it possible for a financial advisor to earn $1 million per year – year in and year out – is readily available, if you know where to look and are willing to make the effort to excel. So, let's consider the secret of sourcing new affluent clients made real by the Elite 1200.

The Secret

Our focus and what we're going to concentrate on is the predominant methodology – the consistently most effective way – the Elite 1200 garner new affluent clients. While many of the Elite 1200, like the vast majority of other financial advisors, employ a wide variety of methods to acquire new well-heeled clients (see *Chapter 4, Acquiring New Affluent Clients*), they have all built strong relationships with other non-competing professionals who provide them with a steady stream of high-quality, pre-qualified, wealthy referrals. The principal non-competing professionals they partner with are accountants and attorneys. That's the secret.

Not much of a secret, is it? We all know that accountants and attorneys, as well as other types of professionals, can be excellent referral sources. In fact, we're very confident that from nearly the time you first started in the business, you caught onto the business-building value of creating relationships with "centers of influence." However, we're not talking about creating a strategic alliance, the most common state of relationships between financial advisors and other professionals. What we are talking about is creating a meaningful strategic partnership between you and a carefully chosen select number of professionals – usually attorneys and/or accountants.

Let's get very clear about what we're talking about by dissecting this concept.

The Elite 1200 have:

- *Built strong relationships with other non-competing professionals*

  ◦ A True Partnership means that they are more than just one of a number of financial advisors being recommended; they are the first and often only financial advisor to be recommended. This is the essence of a strategic partnership compared to a strategic alliance.

- *Who provide them with a steady stream of high-quality, pre-qualified, wealthy referrals*

  ◦ Steady stream does not mean once in a while. Instead it tells us that these professionals are actively looking to make referrals.

◦   <u>High-quality...wealthy</u> tells us we're dealing with affluent individuals and families that have money and have needs you can address.

◦   <u>Pre-qualified</u> means that when they are referred, they already are very positively disposed to you as their financial advisor, and the services and products you can provide.

The **secret** is not that you should create relationships with these professionals. The **SECRET** is to employ a **systematic process** for generating that *steady stream of high-quality pre-qualified, wealthy referrals primed to do business with you NOW*. The secret is in following the path that has been paved by the behavior of the Elite 1200, the very advisors whom have cracked the code on how to get a steady stream of referrals.

The ability to source the affluent in this way, almost universally distinguishes elite financial advisors from other financial advisors who are just as technically competent, just as smart, just as motivated, just as committed to doing what's best for the client. Let me say that again, HOW they sourced their clients was THE distinguishing characteristic. In the financial advisory industry, with open architecture pretty much enabling any financial advisor to provide any product or service, and where "proprietary strategies" are generally non-existent, the ability to access the wealthy client is THE determinant of big-time financial success.

We don't mean to discount the interpersonal skills of the financial advisors. Certainly, those financial advisors who are more proficient at managing the affluent client experience will, over time, indeed be more successful. Nor do we want to discount the technical creativity and expertise many financial advisors bring to the table. However, the opportunity to manage the experiences of affluent clients, or to provide them with brilliantly innovative technical solutions, is very limited unless the financial advisor is able to get to them.

All in all, the **SECRET** to becoming a million dollar financial advisor is to systematically source wealthy clients from other professionals.

What This Book Can Do for You

If your objective is to significantly upgrade your practice, to work with wealthier and wealthier clients – and you might want to include institutional clients such as medical practices, partnerships and corporations – then, in this hyper-competitive environment you will probably need to be able to source clients through other professionals. If your objective is to achieve Elite 1200 status, then you will probably need to be able to source clients through other professionals. If you want to maximize your prospecting efforts, then you will probably need to be able to source clients through other professionals.

This book provides a detailed, empirically-derived process that has been refined and perfected in the trenches. It is the best of both worlds. It is based on a sound quantitative study and honed to a fine point in the hyper-competitive battle for the wealthy. It's a process that, when adroitly implemented, can turbo-charge a financial advisor's annual income – can be the catalyst to Elite 1200 status. In one-to-one coaching of financial advisors employing this process, we find that once they create a mere three to five strategic partnerships, **their incomes rise by at least 40%**. Moreover, their incomes continue to increase at a meaningful rate, until they are pocketing at least $1 million per year.

Herein, we begin with a brief overview of the private wealth market today. The overview provides perspective in the form of size and scope, as well as the core characteristics of the wealthy and their high-net-worth personalities. We want to ensure we all have a solid understanding of the wealthy.

We then discuss the research on sourcing the affluent, as well as taking a more detailed look at the Elite 1200 for they tend to have the critical traits you would want to emulate in order to match their pecuniary success. In many respects, what we have here is a "best practices" prospecting methodology. Subsequently, we look at the nature of their strategic partnership process and the "Five Strategic Shifts" you'll probably have to make to some degree in order to create a pipeline of new affluent clients. Finally, we detail the activities and steps that transform the concepts into business.

We'll show you how to conduct a Professional Profile of your potential strategic partner. We'll plot with you your path down the implementation roadmap. We'll provide you with concepts and numerous examples so you can provide indirect financial incentives to your strategic partners, the "Economic Glue" that bonds these partnerships. Finally, we'll introduce you to *strategic scenario sessions* and *non-aligned structured seminars*. These techniques have proven quite powerful in filling the pipeline with new affluent clients.

What Can Derail Your Success

Creating strategic partnerships the way we're outlining them can, without question, be instrumental in enabling you to work with clients of great wealth. In coaching financial advisors on this methodology, we've found that those who follow the approach diligently and intently become very successful. Unfortunately, they're in the minority.

Brian, for example, grabbed onto the process. Within six months he was introduced to eight affluent investors. The investor with the fewest investable assets was a client with $12 million. From the eight investors, he collected $74 million over the course of a year. Clearly, the approach was working well. However, at about this point in time, Brian attended a seminar that offered a quicker way to cultivating the wealthy. He dropped the RainMaker process in favor of this other approach. Like most financial advisors we've seen, he didn't drop it intentionally, but rather by neglect, due to the attention directed at the new initiative. His new approach did not result in new clients but it was much easier to implement.

It's not uncommon for financial advisors to implement one process and, once that process starts bearing fruit, then jump to another one. For some other financial advisors, the problem is that creating strategic partnerships requires some real work and they're just not up to the task. In Brian's case, both of these were issues.

What you have to recognize is that there's nothing magical about this methodology. This approach is not a paradigm shift. There's no thinking outside the box. On the contrary, the real magic and power of RainMaker, of creating a pipeline of new affluent clients by creating strategic partnerships, is that it's very likely you've already done the heavy lifting. This methodology is predicated on what you probably do exceptionally well already. If you're already consultative with your clients, then all we're doing is showing you how to apply that skill set with professionals who do not do what you do, but who do have wealthy clients who can benefit from your products and services.

So, in the end, what we find derailing the success of financial advisors is that they choose not to succeed, by failing to intention success. They're unwilling to make the effort to ratchet up their practice. The gravitational pull of their entrenched behavior ultimately pulls them down, and back to the ground. So, if you want to excel, if you want a steady stream of new very wealthy clients well primed to do business with you, if your want to make a million dollars or more each and every year, then this book is for you.

Conclusions

Learning from the most successful – in any endeavor – is a very powerful way to improve. For financial advisors, leveraging the time tested expertise of the best financial advisors – the Elite 1200 – is a very powerful way for them to significantly grow their businesses.

A critical success factor for the Elite 1200 is the ability to access affluent clients. Their *secret* is sourcing these wealthy clients through "centers of influence." By "centers of influence," we're not only talking about attorneys and accountants but most any professional who can, on a highly favorable basis, introduce you and/or your expertise to a wealthy client. Nevertheless, attorneys and accountants prove to be – for most of the Elite 1200 – the optimal "centers of influence."

What sets the Elite 1200 apart from the greater majority of financial advisors, who are also seeking to source wealthy clients through "centers of influence," is that they're systematic and process driven. For most financial advisors, the regression from systematic to happenstance is all too real. For most advisors, it's hit-or-miss. For the Elite 1200, it's hit, hit, hit.

If you want to join the ranks of the Elite 1200, then becoming a rainmaker by becoming adept at the process of building and maintaining strategic partnerships is the answer. What's so nice about this process is that most financial advisors already have the requisite skills and talents.

All we're addressing here is how to apply those skills and talents in a slightly different way.

As we noted, in order to achieve Elite 1200 status you'll have to center your business on affluent clients. In the next two chapters, we'll examine this highly lucrative market.

Chapter 2

The Affluent

"A champion needs a motivation above and beyond winning."
– Pat Riley

The private wealth market for the overwhelming majority of financial advisors is the primary, if not exclusive, route to Elite 1200 status. Overall, for financial advisors as well as financial institutions, the wealthy constitute "ideal clients."

The attraction of the affluent is so strong because:

- The private wealth market is highly profitable for financial advisors.

- The wealthy are here to stay.

- The private wealth market is large and growing.

- The affluent turn to financial advisors.

- The private wealth market remains wide-open territory.

Let's take a closer look at each of these issues.

The Private Wealth Market is Highly Profitable for Financial Advisors

We're often asked how profitable the financial advisory business with the affluent can be. The answer is – it depends. The answer has several parts and depends on the array of services and products you are ready to provide to your wealthy clients.

Let's begin by considering the issue from the perspective of life insurance. Affluent clients are exceptionally financially rewarding for financial advisors focused on life insurance. Among the wealthy segment, there is an enormous pent-up (and unrecognized) demand for life insurance. This means that from the demand side perspective, the market has every potential for being highly profitable.

Among affluent clients, life insurance is an excellent solution to estate planning issues. While we're presuming continuation of some level of federal tax on large estates, we will still have many states with their own estate taxes, as well as the continuation of the gift tax and the possibility of the elimination in step up in basis, which would actually open up many more people to having to pay a tax down the line.

In order to look at the potential profitability of the segment from a life insurance perspective, we did a study of estate planning practices among the affluent. In this study of 652 affluent families with estates of $5 million or more, about half (54.3%) had estate plans (Exhibit 2.1). Already, we have identified a significant opportunity; certainly anyone without an estate plan has not thought through the problem of estate taxes and the solution of life insurance. According to this logic, about half of the wealthy (45.7%) are potential prospects for life insurance. Surprisingly, we have actually run into a billionaire without an estate plan.

It turns out that the opportunity is even bigger than these numbers indicate. Not all of these estate plans are up to date. Of those with estate plans, just 16.9% of these plans were completed in the last year, 32.5% were completed between one and five years ago, and the remaining 50.6% were completed over five years ago (Exhibit 2.2). Based on these numbers, it is clear that many of these estate plans are out of date and, therefore, represent opportunities for new estate plans and a new look at insurance needs, at a minimum offering the potential to 1035 the existing policy. This look at estate plans makes a strong, but indirect, case for the attractiveness of the private wealth market. Can an equally strong case be made on the life insurance evidence?

Exhibit 2.1: Have Estate Plans

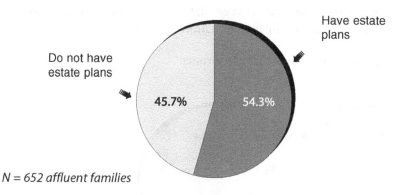

N = 652 affluent families

Source: Creating a Pipeline of New Affluent Clients (2003).

Exhibit 2.2: When the Estate Plan Was Completed

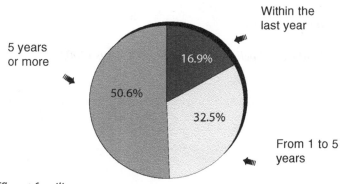

N = 652 affluent families

Source: Creating a Pipeline of New Affluent Clients (2003).

It turns out that looking at the life insurance purchasing data does make a strong case for targeting the private wealth market. In the survey, we found that more respondents actually purchased life insurance than had estate plans (66.9% of the sample had life insurance; Exhibit 2.3). However, like the situation with their estate plans, these purchases were generally done some time ago, meaning that there are still significant opportunities for life insurance sales (Exhibit 2.4). About half of the wealthy (49.8%) bought life insurance over five years ago. Another 32.8% bought life insurance between one and five years ago. The remaining 17.4% purchased life insurance within the last year.

Exhibit 2.3: Have Purchased Life Insurance

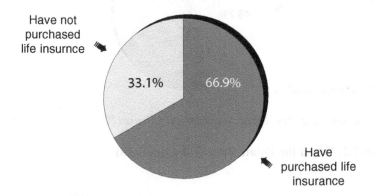

Have not purchased life insurnce
33.1%
66.9%
Have purchased life insurance

N = 652 affluent families

Source: Creating a Pipeline of New Affluent Clients (2003).

Exhibit 2.4: When the Life Insurance Was Purchased

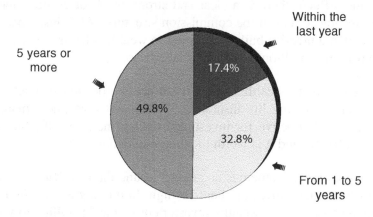

N = 436 affluent families

Source: Creating a Pipeline of New Affluent Clients (2003).

Not only is it most probably the case that their estate plans (for those who have them) are out of date, the amount of life insurance they purchased is inadequate to meet their needs. Just consider the fact that 96.6 percent of these wealthy people report that they are wealthier now than when they purchased the life insurance (Exhibit 2.5).

Exhibit 2.5: Are You Wealthier Since the Life Insurance Was Purchased

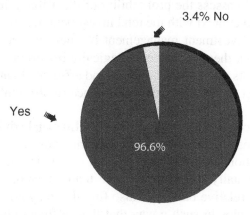

N = 436 affluent families

Source: Creating a Pipeline of New Affluent Clients (2003).

This study (and numerous other ones that validate it) shows that among the affluent there is a clear and strong need for estate planning and life insurance. Given the commission structure of life insurance, we conclude that a practice built on catering to wealthy clients is a sure-fire way to become a million dollar financial advisor.

So the private wealth market is attractive for financial advisors focusing on marketing life insurance. What about investment management? It's also attractive for investment management, but the business model is different and it is worth looking at in detail.

In our experience, there is no getting around the fact that the cost of getting new affluent investor clients is high. In our studies, we find that the first year with a new wealthy investor entrusting $1 million to you is often "revenue-neutral," meaning that the time and expenses you had to invest in getting the client and delivering initial services offsets the fees received. We find that profitability does not take off until year two and sometimes not until year three. However, once your investment advisory business is established, the long-term potential for increasing revenue per affluent investor, and the potential for leveraging each affluent investor relationship, is quite high. In investment management, the retainer-like nature of the private wealth management business is one of its most significant characteristics, and one of its most attractive qualities.

Another way to assess the profitability of the affluent investor market is to look at it in context with the total investment management sector. If we look at the investment management business in general (Exhibit 2.6), we can see that there are three strategically important categories of clients – retail clients, institutional clients, and affluent clients – and they are sensitive to cost and investment performance to different degrees.

When we benchmark against the very best financial advisors providing investment management services, we find that they have a process for managing the relationship with their affluent clients in such a way that their clients are actually *less cost sensitive* than either retail or institutional clients, on a relative basis. We also find that they are able to manage client relationships in such a way that their affluent clients are also relatively *less investment performance sensitive*.

Retail clients, on the other hand, are known for their sensitivity to investment performance as well as their attention to cost issues. Affluent clients are more attractive than institutional clients, who tend to be highly sensitive to pricing considerations and moderately to highly sensitive to investment performance. Like you, thousands of financial advisors have looked at these choices and made their pick. After all, which type of client would you prefer to work with?

Exhibit 2.6: Attractiveness of the Affluent Investor Segment

Factors	Retail Investor	Institutional Investor	Affluent Investor
Price Sensitivity	Moderate	High	Low
Investment Performance Sensitivity	High	Moderate - High	Low

The key is that the ability of the financial advisor to adroitly manage the expectations and experiences of the affluent enable the advisor to not be judged entirely on the client's investment returns on a quarterly basis. This in no way negates the central importance of delivering the very best in the way of investment performance, but it does permit financial advisors to focus on a client's agenda, not just chasing returns.

The Wealthy are Here to Stay

There is yet another reason to concentrate on the private wealth market. Simply put, the wealthy will always be with us. Through economic booms and economic busts, we see that there has always been a monied class. Although their numbers have ebbed and flowed with changes in the economy, throughout history, there has always been and always will be an economic elite.

The outlook for wealth accumulation is good; the baby boomers are entering their peak earning years, the United States economy has become globally competitive, and the spread of free market economies worldwide has created many more opportunities to become rich. And, as long as there have been wealthy people, there have been financial advisors, necessary to assist them in managing their financial affairs.

Although these reasons to target affluent investors should be compelling, there are still other reasons to focus a financial advisory business on the affluent segment. One reason is the sheer size of the opportunity. There are a lot of wealthy people in the world, and in the United States, the wealthy are getting wealthier, and the number of people considered wealthy is growing (see below).

Wealthy Clients Place a High Value on Financial Advisors

Because of the complexity of their financial lives, as well as their desire for control over their lives (see *Chapter 3, Understanding the Affluent*), great numbers of the wealthy seek out and make extensive use of financial advisors. When we examined the decision to use a financial advisor to manage their investable assets, we found that consistently financial advisors were responsible for about 90% of their monies (Exhibit 2.7). Not only that, the wealthier the investor, the greater was their use of financial advisors.

Exhibit 2.7: Percentage of Investable Assets With a Financial Advisor

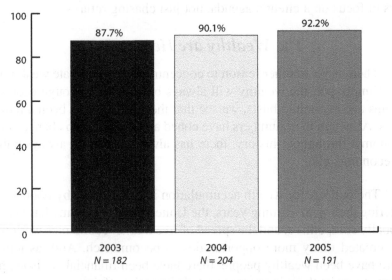

Source: Merrill Lynch Investment Managers/Prince & Associates, 2003 – 2005.

Summing up, what we have found is that the more the wealth, the greater the need to turn to and rely on experts. It's no surprise that the affluent are making extensive use of financial advisors. There is every reason to believe this trend will only increase going forward.

The Private Wealth Market is Large and Growing

Of all the reasons for financial advisors to pursue the affluent market, the most compelling is the sheer size of the market. All over the globe, and all over the United States, the private wealth segment is a large, and growing, market. Whether you look at the aggregate amount of assets or the aggregate number of wealthy people, the numbers are up. These data mean that the private wealth market is structurally attractive.

We empirically ascertained the size of the private wealth market globally. When considering the size and scope of the wealth market, we did not limit ourselves to United States citizens, in part, because the United States is a magnet for the assets of the wealthy from the world over. As one of the most stable and open countries in the world, the United States attracts the monies of wealthy people from other countries. These wealthy individuals all have needs affected by this country's tax laws and related regulations. This translates into considerable business for U.S.-based financial advisors.

Sizing the private wealth universe, and especially the affluent for attractiveness to financial advisors, is an exercise in structural modeling because there is no definitive list of the world's affluent. They stay under the radar if possible. Estimates abound, but most are hamstrung by the fact that the affluent go to great lengths to stay out of the limelight.

There are a number of approaches to creating models that enable us to get our hands around the magnitude of the world of the wealthy. Moreover, there are a number of financial institutions, think tanks, consultancies and the like that strive to provide this data. We're going to note the *2005 World Wealth Report* that considers the matter from the perspective of affluent investors. Then we'll turn to our own efforts in the field. We model the world of the wealthy from the perspective of their total asset/liability picture – their net worth.

There are a number of different estimates of the size and scope of the private wealth market. According to the *2005 World Wealth Report* produced by Merrill Lynch and CapGemini, there are 8.3 million people in the world with a minimum of $1 million in financial assets (i.e., investable assets). This breaks down to 7.4 million people with between $1 million and $5 million in investable assets, 744,800 people with between $5 million and $30 million in investable assets and 77,500 with more than $30 million in investable assets.

More telling was that this is an increase of about 7.3% over 2003. Furthermore, these wealthy individuals control $30.8 trillion in financial assets, an increase of 8.2% compared to 2003.

Let's look at the matter from a slightly different perspective. Instead of just considering financial assets, let's consider their wealth – in other words – their net worth.

The analytic model we'll be detailing here is centered on a more elite and rarified segment of the private wealth universe – those with a net worth of $10 million is the starting point. The model used as its foundation, a previous analytic model we developed that calculated the dimensions of the private wealth universe worldwide (see *Advanced Planning with the Ultra-Affluent: A Framework for Professional Advisor*). We updated that model taking into account the actual and perceived differential when it came to selected assets, including business interests, real property, and collectibles. Furthermore, and of extreme importance, in the current model, we also took into account the impact of the role of the "underground economy" on private wealth creation. With respect to the underground economy, we limited our analysis to "tax avoidance" and related activities. Wealth *created* through illegal activities such as drug dealing and the like was not included as inputs in the model.

The analytic model allows us to create a number of possible estimates. In each case, there is a best estimate, a low-end estimate, and a high-end estimate. Prior to examining the estimates in detail, let's first delineate the sub-categories within the broader category of exceptional wealth (Exhibit 2.8).

Exhibit 2.8: Levels of Affluence

Level	Wealth
Low-end exceptional wealth	$10M to $50M
Mid-range exceptional wealth	$50M to $100M
High-end exceptional wealth	$100M and more

Source: Inside the Family Office (2004).

We're using $10 million in net worth because these families tend to have significant investable assets and they tend to be very good candidates for wealth management services and/or advanced planning services. Moreover, when financial advisors appropriately concentrate their efforts on accountants and private client attorneys, this $10 million number proves to be a very good starting point.

Looking worldwide, our best estimate is that there are 1,104,000 families with US$10 million or more in total assets (Exhibit 2.9). The greater majority are at the low-end with 797,000 wealthy families, while we estimate that there are 231,000 mid-range families and 76,000 at the high-end.

Exhibit 2.9: The Number of Affluent

Level	Low-end estimate	Best estimate	High-end estimate
Low-end	641,000	797,000	1,062,000
Mid-range	202,000	231,000	287,000
High-end	69,000	76,000	79,000
Total	912,000	1,104,000	1,428,000

Source: Inside the Family Office (2004).

As for their wealth, our best estimate is that they control more than $89.7 trillion (Exhibit 2.10). The low-end, though the biggest group by far, controls $21.5 trillion compared to $16.4 trillion for the mid-range group, and an impressive $53.8 trillion, well over half of the total, for the high-end wealthy (even though we capped high-end wealth at $2.4 billion for methodological purposes, we're well aware that there are more than a thousand wealthy families that exceed that cap). In sum, those at the very tip of the wealth pyramid are as far from the low-end affluent as the low-end affluent are from the garden-variety millionaire. Even among the wealthy we find affluence to be bifurcated and weighted to the high-end.

Exhibit 2.10: The Aggregate Wealth of the Affluent*

Level	Low-end estimate	Best estimate	High-end estimate
Low-end	$12.2 Trillion	$21.5 Trillion	$33.9 Trillion
Mid-level	$13.5 Trillion	$16.4 Trillion	$21.2 Trillion
High-end	$41.5 Trillion	$53.8 Trillion	$57.7 Trillion
Total	$67.2 Trillion	$91.7 Trillion	$112.8 Trillion

* For methodological purposes, we capped exceptional wealth at US$2.4 billion, recognizing that there are many exceptionally wealthy families that exceed this number.

Source: Inside the Family Office (2004).

Looking only at the United States, we see that our best estimate is that there are 671,000 families with a net worth of $10 million or greater (Exhibit 2.11). We then proceeded to gauge the aggregate wealth controlled by these affluent families. Again, for methodological purposes, we capped the amount of private wealth any one affluent family can have at $2.4 billion. Once again, we considered a best case, worst case and most likely calculation (Exhibit 2.12).

Exhibit 2.11: The Number of Affluent in the United States

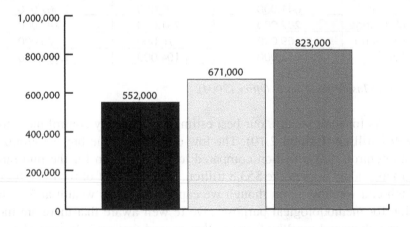

**Exhibit 2.12: Aggregate Wealth Controlled by the
Affluent in the United States**

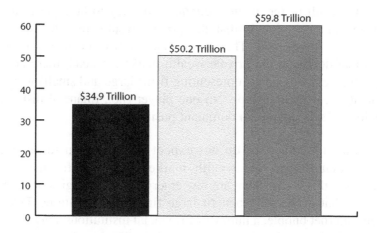

What we can clearly see, both from the *2005 World Wealth Report* as well as our own analytic model, is the enormous and growing opportunity that the private wealth market represents to financial advisors. It's not really the issue of there being wealthy people in need of the services of high-quality financial advisors. It's more an issue of accessing the affluent – which is why you're reading this book.

The Private Wealth Market Remains Wide-Open Territory

There is wide-open territory in the affluent market at this time. There is ample room for the individual financial advisor and the financial advisory team. The principal reason this is so is because wealthy client loyalty predominantly attaches to the individual financial advisor and not to the institution. Wealthy clients generally value their interpersonal/professional relationships far, far more than institutional relationships per se.

Because loyalty is predominantly to the individual, there are relatively low barriers to entering the private wealth advisory business. This market is one that most technically trained financial advisors could (theoretically) enter. The barriers are those of effort, expertise, and contacts, not those of infrastructure costs such as technology. While this is good news for you, it also means many of your colleagues could also seize the same opportunity.

The result of the affluent clients' tendency to be loyal to a person and not an institution is that the private wealth industry structure is extensively fragmented. There is no one, or two, or even a handful of firms that dominate the private wealth market. Instead, there are many, many financial advisors (representing firms large and small) who vie for affluent client relationships. No one player (i.e., financial institution or provider of services) has a dominant position.

Looking ahead, we do not expect this situation to change. We project that the private wealth market will stay fragmented. The reason for this is that there are few emerging technologies or economies of scale that exclusively benefit large financial institutions. During the recent Internet bubble, a number of financial institutions sought to generate scale by leveraging the Internet. As they discovered, the wealthy want to deal with talented people, not technology. This fact very much limits the ability of any financial institution to dominate the business.

Some people point out that the financial advisory business is driven by technology. To a large extent this is true. But the fact remains that the technology is back-office. It remains the interpersonal relationships between financial advisor and high-net-worth client that prove to be the cornerstone to success. We find, over and over again, that it is "client-facing" activities that produce positive results.

Conclusions

We looked at a number of factors that verify focusing on the affluent to be a wise decision for financial advisors. By sheer numbers and persistency, their inherent profitability, their preference to turn to professionals, and the fact that no one financial institution, let alone financial advisor, has a dominant position in the affluent market makes it a field of gold for anyone who knows how to mine it.

With the affluent as our core client target market, it's essential for your success that you're intimately familiar with them. In the following chapter, we provide a brief overview of two key frameworks that provide critically important insights of the affluent.

Chapter 3

Understanding the Affluent

"The will to win is meaningless without the will to prepare!"
— Joe Gibbs

In order to be successful in working with the affluent (that is, to be able to personally earn $1 million or more per year), you have to be competent at working with the wealthy. While we find most financial advisors to be technically proficient, many of them fail to develop the requisite high level of rapport needed to excel. The sales people at Wal-Mart and Bergdorf Goodman are equally adept at ringing up the cash register, but only one provides the service level expected by the wealthy.

Predicated on the research we conducted on the affluent in conjunction with extensively coaching financial advisors, especially high-end financial advisors, we have found the two following frameworks to be extremely potent in enabling financial advisors to be more efficacious with the wealthy. Moreover, for our purposes here, these two frameworks will enable you to gain perspective that comes in quite handy when sourcing the affluent from "centers of influence."

First, we'll address the five core characteristics of the wealthy. Then we'll turn our attention to understanding their high-net-worth personalities. We'll conclude the chapter by showing the integration of the two frameworks.

The Five Core Characteristics of the Wealthy

The affluent are distinguished, first and foremost, by their wealth. Research, confirmed by experience, shows that they also have in common five core characteristics that relate to the way they think of and use their wealth.

The five core characteristics are complexity, control, connections, capital, and charity. Of course, beyond these core characteristics, the affluent are as distinct and diverse as any group of individuals.

Complexity. Simply stated, the fact that the affluent have more money makes their personal and financial lives more complicated. External macro-environmental factors such as tax and estate laws naturally play a far larger role in their lives than they do in other people's lives. In fact, the very policies that constrain them also create significant complexity. The challenge of investment management is an example of complexity at work. Diversification is relatively easy to achieve with smaller portfolios, but for a multi-million dollar portfolio with global exposure, proper diversification is extremely complex, requiring an intricate balance of investments and tax trade-offs.

The affluent generally tend to want to structure their assets to maximize value and ensure preservation and, along the way, they will confront complicated financial issues ranging from dealing with embedded capital gains to, speaking hyperbolically, deciding how much to pay in taxes. Globalization has also produced an environment where many of the affluent confront tax and related financial issues that are multi-jurisdictional, creating a quagmire of international entanglements.

That goes for affluent foreign nationals, as well – a highly desirable market. Consider the case of the wealthiest segment of the Chinese in Hong Kong. Denied British passports when the colony reverted to the People's Republic of China in 1999, they moved assets by the billions out of Hong Kong. California and Canada were initially big beneficiaries of this transfer of assets, but now a significant amount of that money is returning to China in the form of investments by those families in traditional and new asset areas. The investors are, for example, buying back their traditional lands and re-establishing their businesses (or starting new ones) to take advantage of political and economic restructuring.

The back-and-forth creates a maze of legal and tax issues that have to be sorted through, usually requiring the services of professional advisors.

Another area of intense complexity is created by family and personal dealings. The family dynamic is ever-complicated, and money often magnifies eccentricities and animosities. With many voices weighing in, the affluent often have to settle for accommodation rather than optimization. Keeping peace within a family, for example, can override the best course of action for transferring a family business. There are many, many examples of these family systems that play out in the courtrooms and the pages of the tabloid press.

Control. Money and power walk hand in hand, so it is no surprise that the affluent are often focused on ensuring appropriate levels of control. They want to exercise a measure of control or influence over just about every situation of significance in their lives. By the same token, a healthy ego born of success in the business world, or just the raw power of money leads some of the affluent to believe that their solution to any problem is generally the best way to go.

Needless to say, when the complexity of their lives already referred to meets the need for control head-on, life can be very complicated for the affluent – and for their professional advisors. When, for example, the objective is the perpetuation of the founding fortune, the strategies and tactics that are employed do more than just ensure the tax-efficient transfer and perpetuation of vast wealth. They also create an emotional and cognitive framework in which the benefactors must live. There is a psychological, if not legal, hold on the benefactors that make many of them quite ambivalent about the situation.

While not going on strike, the affluent do exert themselves through intricate avoidance and protective behaviors toward the obstacles that society places before them. And, they usually turn to professional advisors to assist them (see *Chapter 2, The Affluent*). The affluent exert control (and create barriers to uncontrolled contact) by working through their advisors.

In the end, control is demonstrated by the way their wealth is structured, communicating just what the wealth creators think of themselves and others be they family, friends, non-profits, or the government.

Consider the fascination a number of the affluent have with family incentive trusts, certain types of family limited partnerships, and even the way some family offices are organized. All these strategies and tactics are, in the end, simply manifestations of the need to be in control.

Connections. Success for the affluent is not only about money. The Chinese have a word for it, and that word is *guanxi* – connections. It is sometimes said that with the right *guanxi*, the right connections, almost anything is possible. Among the affluent, the judicious application of their contacts is essential in both personal encounters as well as facilitating their business success. These relationships are highly prized and are, therefore, well protected.

What is also evident is that, in general, the affluent have access to significant numbers of influential people. The phrase "six degrees of separation" describes how many nodes on a sociogram a person would need to transcend to meet anyone. However, in the case of the affluent, we are rarely talking about six nodes. One detailed socio-diagramming of a wealthy familial unit not originating in the United States found that it was able to access 91.3% of the local political and business leaders as well as 61.1% of Beltway politicians with no more than three degrees of separation. In sum, where the affluent are concerned, the issue is not only access, but influence. And, in this respect, connections address both their ability to reach out to someone and to get something out of their connections.

Capital. By capital, we do not mean wealth per se, but the way that the affluent use money to define themselves. Capital, in this context, is the ability to deploy resources to make things happen – that is, not money itself, but what money can accomplish.

The Ramaz family is an internationally renowned example of the integration of affluence with capital and personal identity. The way the family deploys its resources in both business ventures and charitable causes reinforces its personal identity. In speaking to members of the Ramaz family, we found that they define themselves based on the way they deploy their wealth, by their use of capital, a mindset similar to senior executives who see themselves reflected in the actions of the company they work for.

Charity. Public policy in the United States since the early 20th century has been to create tax incentives for philanthropic actions, and those incentives, coupled with the genuine charitable impulse of the affluent, have a tremendous impact on the nonprofit sector.

Based on our research, we have found that the affluent are not charitable simply because of the tax incentives and the desire to see their name chiseled in stone as benefactors; they are earnestly looking for ways to "make the world a better place." Admittedly, because of the tax breaks, charitable gifting does benefit the affluent as well as the non-profit organizations they support. Nevertheless, the affluent like the sense of purpose charitable gifting gives them and a number aspire to be philanthropists following in the footsteps of Carnegie and Ford. But in fact, the desire to give comes first, and only then do taxes affect the tactics and strategies for giving.

The experience of the Soloton Society demonstrates the interplay of charity with the other core characteristics. The Soloton Society works with the very high-end of the affluent, and in the 1990s alone it facilitated nearly $6 billion in charitable gifts worldwide. The Soloton Society has found that the complexity of the personal and financial situations of the affluent, combined with a pervasive desire for control and their self-definition tied to capital, results in the preference for private foundations and similar types of charitable gifting strategies.

The High-Net-Worth Personalities

The affluent, as seen through the prism of their five core characteristics, is a distinct market segment. Nevertheless, when it comes to money, there are many different high-net-worth personalities that professional advisors need to adapt to. By understanding the nine high-net-worth personalities, financial advisors are better able to understand and communicate with affluent clients, resulting in stronger and more productive relationships.

The creation of psychographic segments – or personalities – involved using the multidimensional statistical tools of factor and cluster analysis on the body of data collected on the affluent. The following provides an overview of the nine high-net-worth personalities and some of their key attributes.

Family Stewards. The most prevalent high-net-worth personalities, are deceptively simple: they are motivated by the need to protect their families over the long-term. This motivation makes them suitable candidates for a wide range of financial services. Research reveals, however, that there is a complex interplay of psychological factors to contend with. That is because Family Stewards are not only characterized by a high degree of internal control – or the confidence to control their own fate and fortune – but also by a deep distrust of the world.

Family Stewards fear for the safety of their families, and they are highly motivated to organize defenses against external threats. This interplay of the themes of safety and threat have operational implications, implying that Family Stewards can be relatively difficult to approach because a new advisor will often be perceived as an "outsider" unless introduced by a confidant of the affluent individual.

Phobics. The second most prevalent high-net-worth personality is typified by people who, although they are wealthy, dislike thinking about money. This personality also has significant control issues because they do not think they are capable of managing their own financial affairs. While this mindset is relatively pervasive among the high-net-worth personalities, it is extreme in the case of the Phobics. However, Phobics also believe they are not especially capable of effectively managing the advisors they turn to for assistance.

This deep feeling of being out of control over this important aspect of their lives makes this segment suspicious and off-putting. Like Family Stewards, they can be difficult to approach unless someone they really trust introduces you.

Independents. This high-net-worth personality includes people whose primary objective in accumulating assets is to achieve financial independence and the accompanying security. Some want to retire from their financial obligations to play golf or go sailing; others will continue to be involved but value the security of knowing they could leave at any time.

These affluent tend to have a high degree of internal control and they are indifferent to a broad range of external threats if they can be protected from them. In contrast to the other high-net-worth personalities, they believe the world is a relatively benign place – all things considered. Independents are also very open to advanced planning if it is tied to their fundamental goals and beliefs.

The Anonymous. This high-net-worth personality shares with the Family Stewards a distrust of external forces, but to an even greater degree. Anonymous affluent clients are typified by their deep-seated – and sometimes irrational – need for privacy and confidentiality in all of their financial, as well as selected, personal dealings.

In their interior belief system, they fear that the disclosure of information will enable someone or some office to get control over them and their affairs. As a result, they can only be accessed if someone they trust introduces them to you.

Moguls. The affluent with this personality are motivated to accumulate more and more assets in order to achieve personal power (and, by extension, influence if not control). In short, they want to leverage the power conferred by wealth.

Moguls are moderate in terms of optimism/pessimism and introversion/extroversion. From professional advisors, they require an acknowledgement of their power. Importantly, they are motivated to participate in financial advisory services that will demonstrably increase their power.

VIPs. The people with this high-net-worth personality are motivated to accumulate assets and utilize their wealth, in part, to achieve greater status and prestige. This personality prizes the opinion of select others above all else. They are, as a result, more likely to purchase the external symbols of wealth than any other high-net-worth personality. They see such symbols, including jets and private islands, as badges of their exalted status.

This high-net-worth personality is less certain about personal control and, thus, relies more on external resources. They are also comparatively fearful, worrying about threats to their wealth and status. For financial advisors, the job is twofold: reassure them while remaining optimistic about their finances, and also exhibit deference and regard for their status.

Accumulators. This high-net-worth personality seeks to accumulate assets out of an overriding concern for personal financial well-being. Unlike other high-net-worth personalities, Accumulators do not seek to achieve family security or emblems of wealth or power. Instead, their focus is on the continual accumulation and protection of assets as a bulwark against an uncertain future.

Accumulators tend to see threats to their financial well-being from all sides. In addition, people with this high-net-worth personality do not have a great deal of confidence in their ability to achieve either internal or external control.

Gamblers. Gamblers are high on both internal and external control dimensions. They believe their skills and competence will protect them from all significant threats, they are self-reliant, and they are more inclined to be extroverted.

They view financial affairs as a personal challenge, but one that they are very capable of handling. For instance, in the investment management world, they seek "playmates," people to share their enthusiasm with, and they are by nature optimistic. They look to professional advisors to maximize their self-image (i.e., capital) and help them realize complete control and protection over their asset pool.

Innovators. Innovators are moderately high on both internal and external control dimensions. They believe their analytical capabilities will sustain them and protect them from external threats. And, because of their life-long reliance on their analytic capabilities, they are highly self-reliant and do not delegate any portion of life tasks having to do with analysis.

Unlike Gamblers, they are more inclined to be introverted. They view financial affairs as an analytic challenge, and they look for professionals who will feed them useful information as well as facilitate implementation, avoiding those who try and dominate them without understanding their analytical bent. Innovators who want to understand every detail of financial models will regularly challenge professional advisors. Financial advisors working with this personality need to empathize with their essential values, as well as their belief in control, and their proclivity for minute analysis.

The High-Net-Worth Personalities and Core Characteristics

A meta-framework overlapping the five core characteristics of the affluent and the high-net-worth personality model provides insights useful in working with the wealthy (Exhibit 3.1). As shown, each high-net-worth personality has different complexity, control, connections, capital, and charitable attributes and needs.

Exhibit 3.1: The Interplay of the Core Characteristics and the High-Net-Worth Personalities

HNW Personalities	Complexity	Control	Connections	Capital	Charity
Family Stewards	Family political dynamics significant	Current controlling generation resists succession	Principal connections are family ties – easiest to leverage horizontally	Need to maintain family control over the business	Desire to make a better world for their children and communicate critical values to them
Phobics	Difficult to manage information flow with this segment	Seeking to replace control with trust	Well-qualified social network of peers	Highly oriented towards conservation of capital	Want results without attending to financial and legal details
Independents	Complex because not always available for decision-making	Seek control over personal activities and autonomy	Prefers few good friends and business associates to many acquaintances	Conservation of capital needs outweighs investments	Tied to instruments that help them assure their goal of personal financial independence
Anonymous	Difficult to manage because of security concerns	Need highest control over privacy and confidentiality	Network limited but tight	Privacy needs drive investment decision-making	Seek to preserve anonymity in giving
Moguls	Will tolerate complexity in planning and management	Highest control needs of all the segments	Network focused downward so power can be exerted	Highly oriented towards new investments (more control opportunities)	Another avenue they can use to exert power and influence

Exhibit 3.1: (continued)

HNW Personalities	Complexity	Control	Connections	Capital	Charity
VIPs	Need for public recognition creates complexity	Need control over personal persona and reputation	Network focused upward, in direction of aspiration; social ties shallower	Will invest in vehicles that create public image	Another avenue for status, prestige and public recognition
Accumulators	Vast and diverse holdings create complex situations	Demand high levels of control and frequent reporting	Medium network; heterogeneous in character	Will accept investment if capital conservation objectives met	Not highly charitably oriented
Gamblers	Complexity created by need for intense communications and quick reaction time	Seek a wide variety of opportunities, not control	Moderate network characterized by intense interaction and shared passions	Most risk-tolerant of all segments, highly investment oriented	Often directly connected to financial returns
Innovators	Very technically demanding, require complex solutions	Will not relinquish control over advanced planning	On introverted side, limited social network; concentrated network; concentrated professional network	Will trade off capital conservation for investment	Interested in new financial solutions as well as creative programs

Source: Advanced Planning with the Ultra-Affluent (2002).

Conclusions

In the United States, with at least 671,000 prospective affluent clients with greater than $10 million in investable assets, and controlling $50.2 trillion in assets, there is a pronounced opportunity for adroit, focused financial advisors to provide valuable services and products. At the very same time, these wealthy families can prove quite rewarding for those financial advisors who are selected to help them.

What you need to do is understand the wealthy at both a strategic and tactical level. Familiarity with the five core characteristics and with the nine high-net-worth personalities provides an effectively proven strategic perspective. However, before you can be of service to the affluent, you must be able to access them.

In the final analysis, your ability to – on a highly favorable basis – connect with an affluent individual is absolutely the most important factor in the success of your practice. Hence, we now turn to the research on how the affluent find their financial advisors.

Chapter 4

Acquiring New Affluent Clients

"Don't measure yourself by what you have accomplished, but by what you should have accomplished with your ability."
                                                                    – John Wooden

Cynthia has built a solid practice by obtaining new investment management clients from loyal current clients and pre-retirement seminars. Her average new client entrusts about $300,000 with her. This is all, or nearly all, of their investable assets. To date, she has $98 million under fee-based management, but she also has 241 clients. Cynthia wants to significantly increase her assets under fee-based management, but she isn't interested in increasing the number of clients she works with. The answer is wealthier clients, and that means acquiring new more affluent clients differently than what she is currently doing.

David does a great job of cultivating client referrals. On average, one out of every three of his clients introduces him to someone new in a year's time. Each of these prospects who become a client bring David from $500,000 to – at the high-end – $2 million in new assets to manage. This is very good – especially compared to industry averages. However, David feels he and his team are ready to work with much more affluent clients. He wants to be working with wealthy clients who have $10 million or more in investable assets. The problem is that David has discovered that his current referring clients are not going to be able to provide him referrals to investors with this level of wealth. In other words, they can predominantly refer laterally in terms of wealth, hence vaulting upward from his existing client base is difficult.

Both Cynthia and David are doing an excellent job of prospecting. As we'll see, client referrals are the dominant way financial advisors source new business. However, as we'll also see, if you want to work with the very wealthy, client referrals prove limiting.

Undoubtedly, you have your own approach to prospecting; over the years, you have settled on a mix of prospecting strategies that works for you. In fact, every single prospecting approach you use, or can think of, or ever heard about can work. Every last one of them can result in you acquiring a new affluent client. Here is your challenge: Is your prospecting strategy enough to lift you to the ranks of the Elite 1200?

To source affluent clients, there are a wide variety of different prospecting approaches from client referrals to seminars and from cold calling to public relations activities you can employ. Every last one of them can make it possible for you to acquire new affluent clients. Most financial advisors employ a mix of prospecting strategies. Still, the key is to concentrate your efforts on those prospecting strategies that will result in the most cost-effective results as well as the optimal results.

The Importance of Referrals: Recapping the Logic

In study after study of the affluent, we find that they tend to choose their financial advisors because of a referral. Nine out of ten private clients find their financial advisors by asking around. They ask friends, associates and other advisors to suggest someone. We can't say it too often: wealthy clients predominantly find advisors through a referral from either peers or from other advisors. These other advisors are predominantly accountants and attorneys, but not always.

This methodology is so pervasive it seriously throws into question the rationale behind multi-million dollar media campaigns targeting the wealthy. Comparatively few amongst this group are motivated this way and, as mentioned earlier, the wealthy bond with individuals, not institutions. In many cases, for the betterment of the financial institution itself, these institutional resources would be far more effectively spent supporting financial advisors in "client facing" activities. This is not to say that astute use of the media to create the "go-to" brand cannot be a very powerful supporting player. However, it's just that – a supporting player. "Referrals" has the lead. Often the combination of a powerful, well-targeted, media campaign with a well-conceptualized and executed referral generation strategy will produce the best results.

Later in this chapter, we'll provide even greater empirical support for the growing importance of referrals from accountants and attorneys for financial advisors. But first, we want to explore why it is that referrals (whether they're from other clients or from professionals) are consistently the best way to garner new affluent clients.

Just why are referrals so effective in garnering new affluent clients? The answer has a number of components, including:

- The intangibility of the financial services offering.

- The perceived complexity of the financial services offering.

- The desire on the part of the affluent to work with "authorities" coupled with a general inability to identify the "authorities."

Intangibility. From the affluent client point of view, financial services are something of a mystery. The services a financial advisor provides can't be seen or touched or evaluated directly. There is no way a wealthy client can do the side-to-side comparison they might for a stereo system, or road test them as they do when buying a new car. Research shows that when a service is important, and intangible, people will try and reduce their risk of making a bad choice by asking other people's opinion. Think about it – how do you find a new doctor? If you're like most people, you ask around.

Complexity. Wealthy clients believe that their situation is important, unique, and complicated. Because they believe their financial situations are complicated, they invest considerable time and effort to find a financial advisor who is just right for them. The way they do this is to ask around and get referrals to financial advisors especially selected for their ability to handle complexity.

Reliance on "authorities." Since wealthy people believe that their situations are complex, they want an expert – a true authority – to work on their behalf. Using the medical analogy again, if they have a serious medical problem, wealthy patients want the expert specialist to be their doctor, not just the local general practitioner. The best way to find out if a financial advisor is an authority on the unique problems of the wealthy is to get the opinions of other wealthy people or other authorities.

Looking at the situation the way the affluent individual does, we can easily see the importance of referrals. When a wealthy person comes to believe they need a new financial advisor, they ask around and get a referral. The reason they do this is because they can't personally compare the work of one financial advisor to another (intangibility), they think their situation is unique (complexity), and they want the best (reliance on authorities).

The implication is clear. If wealthy clients are finding financial advisors like you through referrals, you need to get into the position of being on the receiving end of these referrals. We will take up the process you can use, but we have to answer another question first. This question is: "What referral source is best?" In other words, what is the optimal prospecting strategy? Let's look at the issue from the perspective of the wealthy investors, middle-class millionaires, and wealthy women.

Wealthy Investors

When 161 wealthy investors were queried as to how they found their primary investment advisor (the one managing the majority of the affluent investors' liquid assets), the majority (68.9%) said it was from accountants or attorneys or other non-competing professionals (Exhibit 4.1).

Exhibit 4.1: Method of Finding Their Primary Investment Advisor

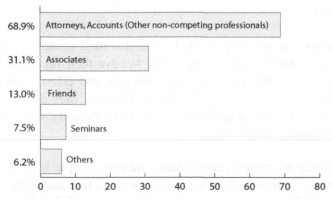

N = 161 wealthy investors

Source: Creating a Pipeline of New Affluent Clients (2003).

In the words of one financial advisor that this data was shown to, his reply can be summarized thusly, "If almost 70% of the wealthy go to their attorney or accountant to find me, why on Earth would I look anywhere else for them?" We have no rebuttal. This is the single most powerful avenue to wealthy referrals. Additionally, it's important to note that 36.6% of this sample group had above $10 million in investable assets. For this group, their reliance on attorneys or accountants or some other advisor to identify for them an investment advisor they should use rose to 89.5%. Clearly, the bigger the client, the more likely they are to go this route.

Middle-Class Millionaires

A substantial segment of the affluent population does not consider themselves wealthy. They strongly identify with being middle class even though they have investable assets ranging from $500,000 to $5 million, as well as a net worth between $1 million and $10 million.

When we look at how middle-class millionaires found their primary financial advisors, the answer is, without a doubt, referrals (Exhibit 4.2). First in importance are referrals from the other professional advisors they employ – accountants and attorneys (54.2%). Then comes a referral from another client of the financial advisor (30.1%). Subsequently, there are a number of other prospecting approaches.

Exhibit 4.2: Importance in Finding Their Primary Financial Advisor

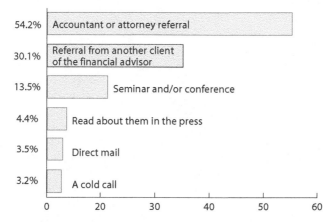

N = 1,417 middle-class millionaires

Source: Cultivating the Middle-Class Millionaire (2005).

Women of Wealth

In a study of 743 wealthy women we found advisor referrals to be the principle way these affluent clients selected a financial advisor. To be eligible for our study, every woman had to meet two criteria:

- They had to have $3 million or more in investable assets. This definition excludes business and real property interests – any assets that are not readily convertible into cash. In the end, comprehensive information was collected from 743 women holding an aggregate of $4.85 billion in investable assets.

- They had to be the principle decision-maker with respect to investment decisions for those assets. That is, they were the primary contact for their financial advisor, and their decisions dictated the actions of their advisor. These women did not share decision making (or defer) to anyone else, including husbands, fathers, sons, or other family members.

When we look at how women of wealth source financial advisors, we find that the answer is referrals. More precisely, they tend to solicit the opinions of attorneys or accountants (Exhibit 4.3). Note that this is the four-lane highway to sourcing new wealthy women clients – professional referrals are used by 69.9% of women of wealth. No other way of locating an advisor even comes close.

Exhibit 4.3: Importance of Each Method in Finding the Person Who is Now the Primary Financial Advisor

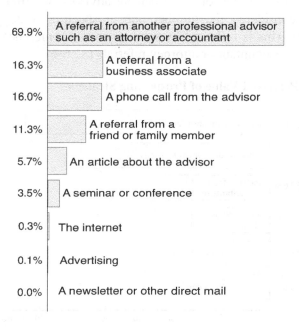

69.9%	A referral from another professional advisor such as an attorney or accountant
16.3%	A referral from a business associate
16.0%	A phone call from the advisor
11.3%	A referral from a friend or family member
5.7%	An article about the advisor
3.5%	A seminar or conference
0.3%	The internet
0.1%	Advertising
0.0%	A newsletter or other direct mail

N = 743 Women of Wealth

Source: Women of Wealth (2004).

Clearly, as seen in these studies, other professionals, notably accountants and attorneys, are the advisors the affluent turn to for advice concerning financial advisors. The question then becomes, what are the financial advisors doing to source the affluent through them?

Financial Advisors

Turning to a survey of 512 financial advisors, we find that client referrals is considered the number one prospecting strategy (74.6%) (Exhibit 4.4). This is followed by seminar and/or conferences (57.4%). Then we have accountant or attorney referrals (37.6%).

Exhibit 4.4: Perceived Value of Prospecting Strategies

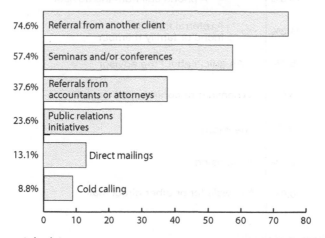

N = 512 financial advisors

Source: Cultivating the Middle-Class Millionaire (2005).

More enlightening, when we turn to the financial advisors, is their response to the question: "In the last 12 months, how did you get your best new affluent client (investable assets of $500,000 or more)?" Now, we see that referrals from accountants and attorneys rule (64.4%) (Exhibit 4.5). For 29.5% of the financial advisors, their best new affluent client came from a referral from a current client. And, 6.1% of the financial advisors sourced their best new affluent client some other way, such as a seminar, or the wealthy client came in over the transom.

Exhibit 4.5: Sourcing Their Best New Affluent Client

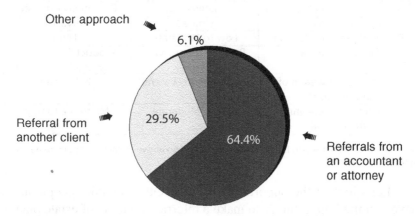

N = 512 financial advisors

Source: Cultivating the Middle-Class Millionaire (2005).

Client Referrals Compared to Professional Referrals

Now, we're not negating the need for you to source new wealthy clients from your current clients. On the contrary, we've developed a number of processes that are very effective in enabling financial advisors to get referrals from their clients (see *The Millionaire's Advisor* and *Cultivating the Middle-Class Millionaire*). It's just that between the two approaches, professionals are easily the better opportunity. By examining client and professional referrals side-by-side, we can see why professional referrals are a more powerful prospecting strategy (Exhibit 4.6).

Take the number of potential referrals. Your other wealthy clients will tend to know a relatively few other qualified potential clients. On the other hand, think of how many affluent clients an attorney or an accountant has. By selecting the "right" professional as your strategic partner, the number of potential affluent clients they will be able to refer to you is considerable.

Exhibit 4.6: Client Referrals Compared to Professional Referrals

Factors	Client Referrals	Professional Referrals
Number of potential referrals	Relatively few	Potentially extensive
Opportunity to refer	Limited	Pervasive
Extent of pre-qualification	Low to Moderate	High
Focus of referral	Product &/or service	Product &/or service &/or needs and wants
Vaulting up in wealth of current clients	Predominantly Lateral*	High Upside
Likelihood of accepting the referral	Low to Moderate	Moderate to High

*For clients with a net worth below $5 Million. As you go above $5 Million, this incrementally fades.

Let's look at the opportunity to refer. Other wealthy people usually have a limited opportunity to make a referral; the topic of estate planning or tax-efficient investing just does not come up in everyday conversation. Circumstances have to be just right for a wealthy person to suggest that you might be the answer to a problem one of their friends is having. Some financial advisors manage to get their clients to do some low level prospecting for them, but this is hard to do in a consistently successful manner. On the other hand, attorneys and accountants are not similarly restricted. In fact, it is their job to be on the lookout for issues that their wealthy clients need resolved and for the experts whose knowledge and skills are necessary. These professionals, by the nature of their professional relationship with their wealthy clients, can introduce you and the work you do into the conversation whenever it is appropriate. Given the situation most of their affluent clients are in, there is almost always an appropriate time.

When it comes to the extent of pre-qualification of your wealthy prospects, the advantage also goes strongly to the professionals. Clients who refer affluent clients usually only have a vague idea of their net worth and/or investable assets. Accountants and attorneys, on the other hand, have extensive knowledge of their affluent clients' financials. More to the point, the attorney or accountant will know if a particular wealthy client is a good referral for you.

Ideally, you want a referral who wants a long-term relationship centered around his or her evolving needs, not someone who just wants one product. Whereas a wealthy client will almost always only talk about a product (e.g., a hedge fund) or a broadly defined easy-to-comprehend service (e.g., retirement planning), professionals can also address the needs and wants of the wealthy client when making a referral. That is, attorneys or accountants will probably have greater insight into their wealthy clients' financial agendas so that they can make a referral by bringing you in to help solve problems.

Clients with less than $5 million in net worth predominantly refer individuals with the same financial demographics. This tends to fade incrementally as the clients become wealthier. On the other hand, referrals from accountants and attorneys will, if you select the "right" professional (see *Chapter 9, The Professional Profiling Tool*), be positioned to introduce exceptionally wealthy individuals to you.

For many financial advisors, the most important distinction between client and professional referrals is the responsiveness of the wealthy person being referred. When professionals make referrals of their affluent clients, there is a very good chance those referrals will turn into new affluent clients for financial advisors (see *Chapter 5, Accountants and Attorneys as Potential Strategic Partners*). The same cannot be said for referrals from your current clientele. Said another way, there is a good chance that someone referred by their attorney or accountant will become a client. The conversion rate when someone is referred by a client is meaningfully lower.

What does this all mean? Affluent client referrals are, and will remain, an important way for you to garner more wealthy clients. However, referrals from professionals – in particular accountants and attorneys – are a far more powerful prospecting approach. The mountains of research all point to one clear answer – building a practice through referrals from professionals is the fastest way to Elite 1200 status. Will it be easy? No. There is competition – lots and lots of competition.

The Competition for Accountant and Attorney Referrals

There is a lot of competition in the field. You are not the first (and you will not be the last) to follow the logical path to get to this point. When you consider the data and listen to the stories of how financial advisors found many of their wealthiest clients, it all comes down to generating referrals from professionals. As we said in *Chapter 1, The Secret to Sourcing New Affluent Clients*, the secret is not much of a secret. No surprise, then, that there is a great deal of competition for these attorney and accountant client referrals.

But not all financial advisors are competing as aggressively, and certainly not as intelligently. Here is how to scope out the competition. In Exhibit 4.7 we find that there is considerable interest among some types of financial advisors for affluent client referrals from professionals, and relatively less among others. Life insurance producers are the most interested (81.6%) while money managers are the least (72.5%). What is clear is that there are certainly many financial advisors who want to "befriend" attorneys and accountants.

Exhibit 4.7: Interest in Garnering Referrals from Lawyers and Accountants

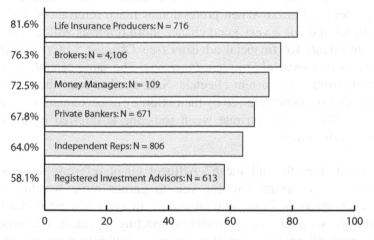

Source: Creating a Pipeline of New Affluent Clients (2003).

The management of financial institutions has similarly recognized the **secret** and 63.9% of them have established a formal value-added or referral program (Exhibit 4.8). These programs are intended to support their financial advisors in creating "strategic alliances" with attorneys and accountants. The life insurance companies have taken the lead in this area; 92.3% of those surveyed have implemented formal referral programs.

Exhibit 4.8: Have a Formal Referral Program for Their Financial Advisors

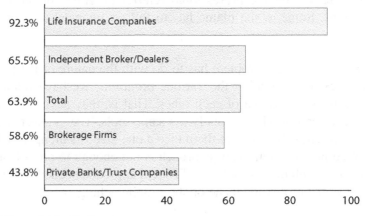

N = 108 financial institutions

Source: Creating a Pipeline of New Affluent Clients (2003).

Unfortunately, not all programs are good programs. In fact, the problem with the programs of the financial institutions is that only 11.9% of financial advisors like them (Exhibit 4.9). The reasons for this are multifarious, yet in the end, they simply have not found them to be productive. More life insurance producers (17.1%) than any other advisor find them very useful, but this is still a relatively small proportion.

Exhibit 4.9: Have Found their Firm's Referral Program Very Useful

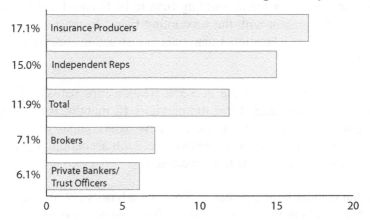

N = 1,551 financial advisors

Source: Creating a Pipeline of New Affluent Clients (2003).

There are many reasons for the lack of success so many financial advisors have with the professional referral programs of the financial institutions. Some of the blame has to fall on financial advisors themselves.

But some of the problem has to do with the nature of the programs themselves. In examining the various programs, we have found many of them to be derivative of each other. That is, they advocate the same approaches and provide basically the same tools. The greatest weakness we uncovered is that most of them take a one-size-fits-all approach. This sort of common denominator approach is not enough to provide a financial advisor with the distinctively different approach needed to garner the interest of the professionals he or she is approaching.

A winning approach has to be customizable to the financial advisor using it and to the targeted professional. We have, therefore, corrected for the weaknesses we found in the referral programs of the financial institutions by developing a systematic process centered on customization.

Formal Partnership Programs for Accountants

Digging a little deeper into this issue, we examined the success of 198 financial advisors across seven financial institutions who participate in their firm's accountant partnering program. On average, each financial advisor established relationships with 18.5 accounting firms. This entailed arranging for the accounting firm to be licensed and having an exclusive arrangement with the accounting firms. In most cases, it also included providing educational materials in instruction concerning financial products.

In total, we were looking at 3,552 relationships between financial advisors and accountants. Over the previous 12 months, these relationships generated nearly $2.3 billion in new assets under management. However, this only means that, on average, each accounting firm generated $640,000 in new assets to be managed.

What is more telling is that 24 financial advisors (12.5%) accounted for 82.6% of all these new assets. These financial advisors working with, on average, three accounting firms brought in $1.9 billion. This translates into $26 million in new assets per accounting firm.

In looking closely at what these financial advisors were doing we found that they were very selective regarding which accounting firms they would do business with. In effect, they conducted a detailed evaluation of their potential accounting partners. This resulted in them concentrating on a very small number of high-potential accounting firms for whom they customized the way they did business. Moreover, they intensely worked those relationships. Most of the 24 financial advisors used a variation of *strategic scenario sessions* (see *Chapter 11, Filling the Pipeline*).

For the vast majority of financial advisors, the partnering programs provided by their financial institutions enables them to formally create the relationship but is lacking in the processes that converts agreement to do business into business. The presumption – that once the accounting firm is licensed and can share in the revenues the accountants will be motivated to conduct financial services business – proved wrong. The problem is that they don't know how few are comfortable with approaching their clients about financial products. So, unless steps are taken to overcome these obstacles, you end up going to a number of lunches with the accountant to discuss and re-discuss and discuss again the same set of issues – how to work together.

Another mistake many financial advisors make, and one that's promoted by many of these programs, is the idea that the more accountants the better. As we can see in these findings, fewer accounting firms, properly selected, is optimal. We refer to this as the law of Small Numbers (see *Chapter 7, Five Strategic Shifts*).

Conclusions

There are lots of ways of prospecting, but only one that will enable you to create a sustainable pipeline of wealthy clients. Nevertheless, in survey after survey of the affluent, we find that they strongly tend to select their primary financial advisors based on referrals from "centers of influence." Whether we're dealing with affluent investors or middle-class millionaire, wealthy women or the various other segments of the high-net-worth market, referrals from trusted advisors are critical to enable you to source new affluent clients.

We've also seen that relatively few financial advisors are proactively leveraging relationships with other professionals to build their own practices. We see this even though these same advisors identify accountants and attorneys as being the source of their best new affluent client within the past year.

What is also clear is that while so many in the industry – including the financial institutions – are interested in "teaming up" with accountants and attorneys, they are doing a woefully poor job. Even where the accountants are financially motivated to work with a financial advisor to provide products, very few of them are what anyone would define as being successful.

In the next chapter, we drill down on the opportunities accountants and attorneys can provide for financial advisors. We'll also touch on some other types of advisors that should not be overlooked.

Chapter 5

Accountants and Attorneys as Strategic Partners

"Setting a goal is not the main thing. It is deciding how you will go about achieving it and staying with that plan."

– Tom Landry

Who has access and influence with the affluent? More to the point, who has access and influence with the affluent and can direct them to you? A little more precisely, who has access and influence with the affluent, can direct them to you and does not compete with you? Anyone who fits this simple description is potentially a strategic partner.

From our perspective, a strategic partner is a professional with affluent clients who doesn't provide the services and/or products you do OR a professional willing to share the revenue from the services and/or products you provide.

This definition opens the door to a considerable number of prospective strategic partners. We've seen that thoughtful financial advisors will indeed move beyond the "traditional centers of influence" to other – mostly untapped – professionals. Nevertheless, as we'll see, you must not overlook those traditional "centers of influence." In particular, for most financial advisors the preferred strategic partners will be accountants and attorneys.

The Opportunities with Accountants and Lawyers

It is widely accepted that attorneys and accountants are the best referral sources for wealthy clients. In fact, as we saw in the last chapter, the affluent readily turn to these professionals and ask for recommendations when they are seeking a financial advisor. Looking at survey data is one way of validating this approach.

What we'll do here is quantify the business opportunity at hand. You will invest considerable resources if you implement this process, and you should satisfy yourself that it will be worth the effort. This is precisely the purpose of these sections.

When it comes to these "centers of influence," we're talking about three types:

- Private client attorneys.

- Accountants (who are not themselves financial advisors).

- Accountants who are financial advisors.

Let's now consider the research about the opportunities that exist with these professionals, starting with private client attorneys.

The Opportunity with Private Client Lawyers

Your target private client attorney is a professional with affluent clients to whom the following services are provided:

- Planning services including but not limited to:

    ° estate planning;

    ° asset protection planning;

    ° income tax planning;

    ° succession planning;

    ° business planning for successful entrepreneurs; and

    ° development of charitable giving programs.

- Administrative services tied to the above planning services.

- Provisioning of opinion letters and related services such as due diligence on selected tax strategies.

- Probate services.

- Guardianship and conservatorship services.

Lawyers are good potential strategic partners because they routinely make referrals so that their wealthy clients can get the investment, banking, and various insurance services that they need.

It turns out that private client attorneys do direct business to financial advisors who provide investment management services. In fact, they refer nearly 10% of their wealthy clients for money management services (Exhibit 5.1). The average amount of investable assets per client referred by an attorney was $2.7 million. We can easily compute the value of these referrals. Financial advisors charge an annual fee of about 1% to manage investable assets. That means that each of these clients is worth an average of $27,000 a year to a financial advisor.

Exhibit 5.1: Referrals to Financial Advisor for Investment Management

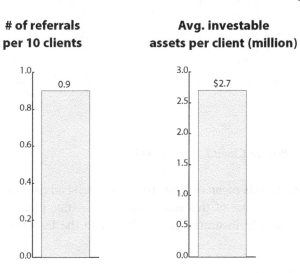

N = 619 attorneys

Source: The Private Client Lawyer (2003).

Lawyers also referred their clients to life insurance producers. Life insurance products are very often a tax-advantaged solution in estate planning for the wealthy. In fact, they made more referrals to life insurance advisors than they did to investment advisors.

Lawyers will refer an average of 2.1 clients for every 10 they have for life insurance products. These clients have an average estate of $8.1 million (Exhibit 5.2).

Exhibit 5.2: Referrals to Financial Advisors for Life Insurance

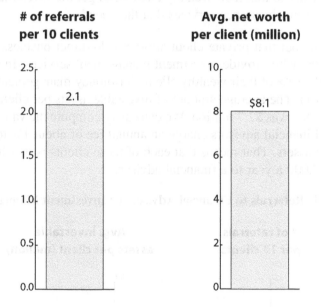

N = 619 attorneys

Source: The Private Client Lawyer (2003).

These referrals mean revenue to the financial advisors who got them. People with an estate of that magnitude need estate planning, and probably could use life insurance as a solution to the tax issue. Legislative changes to the estate tax laws notwithstanding, large estates need estate planning, and life insurance products are frequently indicated solutions. Moreover, these attorneys are also well positioned to refer business owners to financial advisors where life insurance serves business needs such as funding a buy/sell agreement.

As noted, attorneys also make referrals for banking services – in particular credit (Exhibit 5.3). Out of every 10 clients, they refer 0.2 to a bank. The average size of the loan is $24.3 million.

Exhibit 5.3: Referrals to Financial Advisors for Credit

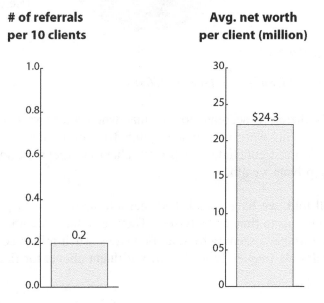

**# of referrals
per 10 clients**

**Avg. net worth
per client (million)**

N = 619 attorneys

Attorneys are an excellent source of referrals, because when the attorney makes referrals to financial advisors, it usually translates into business. In fact, private client attorney referrals resulted in business for the referred financial advisor about three-quarters (73.2%) of the time (Exhibit 5.4). This means that a referral coming from an attorney is likely to be a high-quality, pre-qualified, and motivated prospect.

Exhibit 5.4: Affluent Clients' Use of Referrals

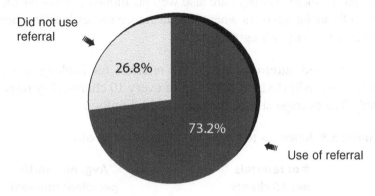

Did not use referral

26.8%

73.2%

Use of referral

N = 619 attorneys

Source: The Private Client Lawyer (2003).

It's therefore accurate to say that when attorneys made referrals affluent clients were very much inclined to follow their recommendations. We must conclude that private client attorneys are influential in moving private wealth.

All told, we have established that attorneys are well positioned to make referrals to financial advisors. They see a lot of wealthy clients and are comfortable screening for qualified cases. Their influence is such that these referrals frequently lead to new affluent clients for financial advisors.

What is evident is that attorneys can indeed be a tremendous source of high-quality referrals for financial advisors. Now, the question is, "How inclined are they to identify referral opportunities? Overall, about one-quarter of the attorneys surveyed were actively looking for eligible clients to refer (Exhibit 5.5). This means that a relatively few attorneys are making the majority of referrals. If all attorneys were to begin actively looking for referrals to make, we could certainly expect a sharp rise in the number of clients streaming to financial advisors.

Exhibit 5.5: Actively Looking to Make Referrals

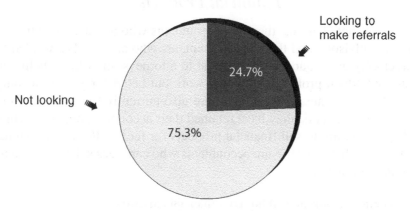

N = 619 attorneys

Source: The Private Client Lawyer (2003).

Let's sum up the case for private client attorneys. With their high rates of referrals, attorneys are already critical players in the professional practices of many financial advisors. Wealthy clients tend to follow through on the recommendations of their attorneys. Private client lawyers can continue to use their influence to send affluent clients (and the revenues they generate) to financial advisors. While some attorneys are themselves becoming financial advisors – a trend known as multidisciplinary practices – this trend is still in its infancy, and may never grow up very much. Finally, there is considerable upside in the finding that a small proportion of attorneys are currently actively looking for wealthy clients to refer.

We conclude that private client attorneys are in a very strong position to benefit financial advisors. The catch is that they are sending only a relatively small number of their wealthy clients to financial advisors. But this is exactly where the opportunity lies. Many more of their affluent clients would significantly benefit by being introduced to the right financial advisor.

Opportunities with Accountants Who Market Financial Products

As we noted above, there are accountants who are also operating as financial advisors, and there are accountants who are not. We wanted to look closely at accountants in contrast to attorneys, in order to help you figure out which professional would work out better for you. In a study of 1,685 accountants, 321 (19.1%) are also currently financial advisors (Exhibit 5.6). That is, they have retained their accounting practices while adding the ability to sell financial products for fees and/or commissions. On the other hand, 80.9% are accountants who earn fees solely from their accounting practices.

Exhibit 5.6: Accountants Who Are Financial Advisors

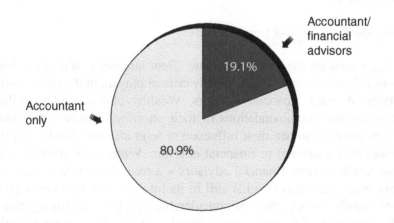

N = 1,685 accountants

Source: Accountants as Wealth Managers (2003).

Many accountants are planning to expand their practices and offer investment management to their clients. It is quite telling that 48.9% of the accountants surveyed anticipate offering financial products within three years (Exhibit 5.7). Experience tells us that many of these accountants who say they are going to be financial advisors will not end up as such. Still, there are a significant number of accountants who are, and who will be, positioned to take fees and/or commissions for the sale of financial products.

**Exhibit 5.7 Accountants Who Will Be
Financial Advisors Within Three Years**

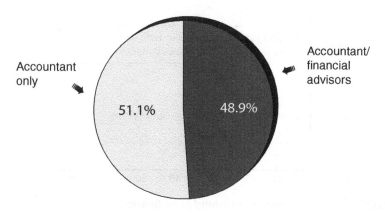

Accountant
only

Accountant/
financial
advisors

51.1%   48.9%

N = 1,685 accountants

Source: Accountants as Wealth Managers (2003).

At first glance, it would seem as though these accountants would represent significant competition to financial advisors. Instead of making referrals, they could keep the wealthy clients for themselves. In fact, that is *not* how accountants are approaching this end of their business. Knowing accountants' motivations is important if you want to develop strategic partnerships with them. They realize that they have to access the expertise of top-flight financial advisors. In fact, two of the most critical success factors for these accountants are: (1) creating strategic alliances with experts in life insurance and/or investments (74.8%) and (2) being able to access financial advisors on a case-by-case basis (70.5%) (Exhibit 5.8). Accountants are getting licensed so they can participate in the income flow, not so they can do the whole job.

**Exhibit 5.8: Critical Success Factors for Accountants
Who Are Financial Advisors**

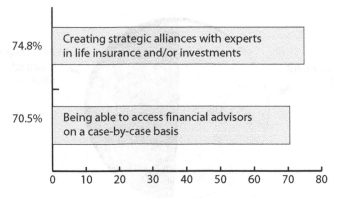

N = 824 accountants who are or intend to be financial advisors.

Source: Accountants as Wealth Managers (2003).

Accountants who appear to be direct competitors can, in fact, be valuable allies. Accountants who want to be compensated from the sale of financial products recognize they need to access the expertise of financial advisors. While the financial advisors will need to share in the revenue, this situation can become win-win. Remember, a smaller percentage of something is far better than 100% of nothing.

Interestingly, there is a sub-segment of accountants, whom would like to fee-share with a financial advisor, but have not found a way to effectively communicate the benefit to their clients, especially with the backdrop reputation as the "client's most trusted advisor." Many variants exist. However, one very successful accountant we know put it this way to his clients as they made the decision, "I have known you for years. I am at the center of your life on all financial issues. I know everything about your financial picture, your personal situation and your goals. If you could have me involved with everything that goes on with your financial advisor at no additional cost to you, why wouldn't you want to do that?"

In our experience, if the impediment to a fee-sharing arrangement is the sole hurdle to overcome, it is often because an accountant doesn't know how to appropriately discuss or disclose fees to their clients. By giving the accountant a beneficial way to frame this situation to their client, you can expedite your route to success.

What is critical for you is not only being able to partner with these accountants but being able to efficaciously access their clientele for your offerings. As we previously noted, just teaming up is woefully insufficient. This problem would be solved if you were to employ the Whole Client Model in the context of *strategic scenario sessions* (see *Chapter 11, Filling the Pipeline*).

Opportunities with Accountants Who Will Just Refer Their Affluent Clients

Our final segment includes accountants who say they do not expect to be offering financial services in the next three years. There are several reasons they cite to explain their decision (Exhibit 5.9). Most feel that entering the financial services field represents an insurmountable conflict of interest (95.4%). Being dedicated to financial and tax analysis and reporting helps them, they believe, maintain their objectivity (a particularly compelling issue in the wake of the Andersen/Enron debacle). More than four out of five did not want to expand their practices because they see themselves as accounting professionals, not insurance or investment specialists (81.5%). Finally, more than three-quarters of these accountants did not want to risk compromising their standing as *the* trusted advisor to their clients (76.5%).

Exhibit 5.9: Reasons for *Not* Being a Financial Advisor

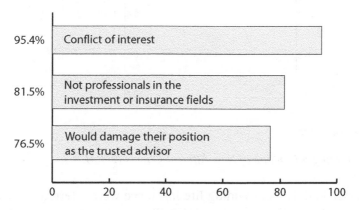

N = 861 accountants who say they will not offer financial services in three years.

Source: Accountants as Wealth Managers (2003).

Financial advisors interested in working with this segment need to respect their rationale for not taking fees and/or commissions. Finding ways to deliver value to referring accountants without creating ethical conflicts will be crucial. The potential of these accountants for financial advisors is high.

As in the attorney section, we will consider referrals from accountants for three products – investment management, life insurance and credit. In a study of 251 accountants who do not take fees and/or commissions on financial products, we see that they refer nearly a quarter of their clients for investment management services. The average amount of investable assets per client was $900,000 (Exhibit 5.10).

Exhibit 5.10: Referrals to Financial Advisor for Investment Management

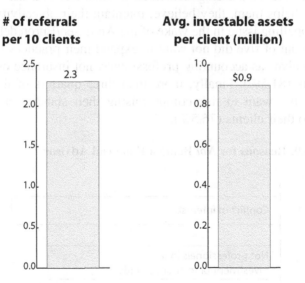

N = 251 accountants

Source: Creating a Pipeline of New Affluent Clients (2003).

Financial advisors providing life insurance were referred to as well. Out of ten affluent clients, accountants will, on average, refer 1.6 of them for life insurance products. These clients had an average estate of $3.4 million (Exhibit 5.11).

Exhibit 5.11: Referrals to Financial Advisors for Life Insurance

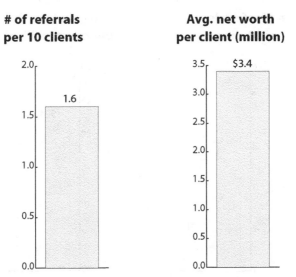

N = 251 accountants

Source: Creating a Pipeline of New Affluent Clients (2003).

These accountants can also be excellent sources of clients – especially business owners – in need of credit (Exhibit 5.12). For every 10 clients, the accountants find they're making 3.8 referrals to bankers for loans. And, on average, each of these loans is for $17.4 million.

Exhibit 5.12: Referrals to Financial Advisors for Credit

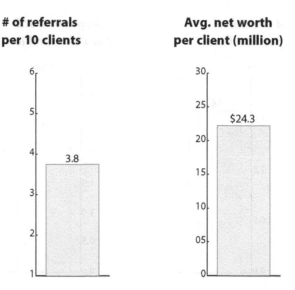

# of referrals
per 10 clients   Avg. net worth
per client (million)

N = 251 accountants

As with attorneys, when accountants make referrals to financial advisors, it usually translates into business. Accountant referrals resulted in business for the referred financial advisor about 60% of the time (Exhibit 5.13). Based on these findings, we can conclude that accountants are very influential with their clients. That makes them very important to financial advisors.

Exhibit 5.13: Affluent Clients' Use of the Referrals

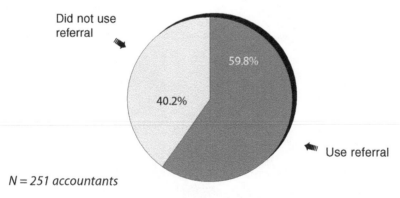

N = 251 accountants

Source: Creating a Pipeline of New Affluent Clients (2003).

In sum, accountants can be an exceptional source of new affluent clients for financial advisors. They are influential, which means that when they do make a referral there is a strong likelihood that the client will follow through and that the financial advisor will acquire a new wealthy client.

There is one aspect to all of this that still needs to be looked at. There is still an open question: "How inclined are accountants to identify referral opportunities?" The answer is "not much." The research shows that just 19.5% of accountants are actively looking for eligible clients to refer (Exhibit 5.14). Right now that creates a problem for the advisor looking for referrals. But if you think in a slightly different way, this finding implies a great, untapped opportunity.

Exhibit 5.14: Actively Looking to Make Referrals

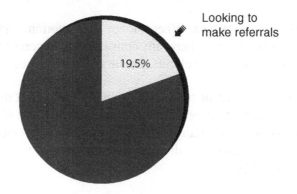

N = 251 accountants

Source: Creating a Pipeline of New Affluent Clients (2003).

Like private client attorneys, accountants who are not going to be financial advisors themselves are – or can be – excellent sources of new affluent clients for financial advisors. So, overall, both accountants and attorneys are "centers of influence" you can tap, resulting in a pipeline of new affluent clients.

Opportunities with Other Types of Professionals

While financial advisors tend to focus on private client attorneys and accountants, as well they should, there are other "centers of influence." Most financial advisors have not made any effort to create any kind of professional relationship with the other professionals listed below, leaving the opportunity to you.

Let's turn our attention to some of these other "centers of influence." We'll be considering:

- Divorce attorneys.

- Executive coaches.

- Family security consultants.

Divorce attorneys. When money is in motion, when circumstances dramatically change, there are considerable opportunities for financial advisors to garner new clients. Divorce is one of those opportunities.

The very idea of trading affluent clients with a divorce attorney is absurd. Imagine talking to one of your wealthier clients and asking him or her: "How's your marriage? I just happen to know an excellent divorce attorney." Nevertheless, divorce attorneys can be very powerful referral sources for you.

Simply put, there are two types of divorce attorneys – those whose practices are focused exclusively on divorce cases and those whose practices include handling divorces as well as other matters. We recommend you concentrate on the former type of divorce attorney. They tend to deal with many more divorce cases and, very importantly, they tend to deal with the wealthy.

A secondary filter in determining the best prospects is to find those attorneys that represent the female in the divorce, more commonly than the male. Why? At the risk of seeming politically incorrect, the statistics show quite clearly that women in the dyad are much less likely to have a solidly established relationship with a financial advisor.

In one survey of 102 dedicated divorce attorneys, we found that 87.3% were asked by more than 10 clients (with $1 million or more in liquid assets) in the previous year for a referral to a financial advisor (Exhibit 5.15). More telling is that 34.8% made referrals to financial advisors (Exhibit 5.16).

Exhibit 5.15: Asked for a Referral to a Financial Advisor

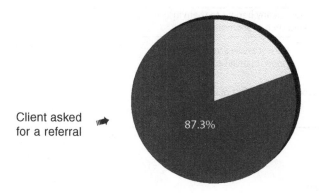

Client asked for a referral ➡ 87.3%

N = 102 divorce attorneys

Exhibit 5.16: Divorce Attorney Referred a Financial Advisor

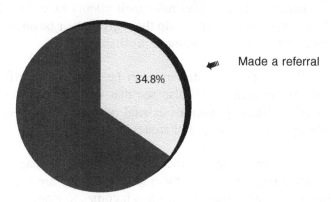

34.8%   ◀ Made a referral

N = 89 divorce attorneys

The primary reason 58 divorce attorneys who were asked by their clients to recommend a financial advisor did not do so was because they did not see any benefit in making such a recommendation (87.9%) (Exhibit 5.17). If the client is happy with the financial advisor … great.

But this will not do much for the divorce attorney's practice. However, the problems that can arise – including legal ones – if the financial advisor referral proves to be a problem, can be considerable.

Exhibit 5.17: Reasons *Not* to Refer a Financial Advisor

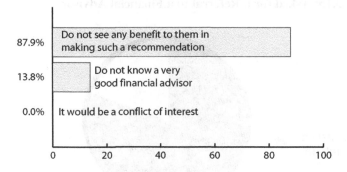

N = 58 divorce attorneys

Among the 31 divorce attorneys who did make referrals to financial advisors, we found that only seven of them (22.6%) would not change the financial advisors they refer their clients to, even if a new financial advisor was able to either help them grow their business by "delivering" new clients or make them more profitable.

Clearly, divorce attorneys can be a source of affluent investment management clients. We also see that very few divorce attorneys have a solid relationship with a financial advisor. Consequently, the divorce attorney is another potential strategic partner for you.

Executive coaches. Increasingly, senior managers are turning to executive coaches to give them an edge. They are seeking assistance in thinking through alternatives when it comes to managing their businesses as well as their careers. At the same time, we're seeing privately held business owners also turning to executive coaches to help in managing aspects of their businesses, as well as the intersection of their businesses and personal lives.

Anyone can call themselves an executive coach (or some similar title) resulting in a great many executive coaches you need to avoid. Only a relatively handful of the literally tens of thousands of executive coaches will have the high quality executive as a client.

In a survey of 83 executive coaches who have at least 10 business owner clients with a minimum net worth of $10 million, we found that only 4.8% have referred their clients to a financial advisor within the last two years. When the 79 executive coaches were asked if their clients could use a high-quality financial advisor for themselves or their businesses, 87.3% said yes. So, with the greater majority of executive coaches recognizing the benefit a high-quality financial advisor would be to their clients, why aren't they recommending someone?

It's the same for executive coaches as it is for divorce attorneys – no identifiable upside and plenty of downside (Exhibit 5.18). About nine out of ten (91.3%) of the executive coaches do not see any benefit to them to make such a referral. Meanwhile, very few (5.6%) do not know a high-quality financial advisor and only 2.9% see making such a recommendation as a conflict of interest.

Exhibit 5.18: Reasons *Not* to Refer a Financial Advisor

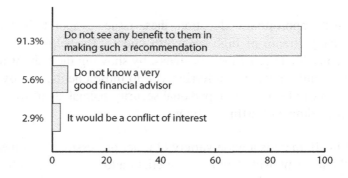

N = 69 executive coaches

Family security consultants. More than ever before the wealthy are employing the services of personal security specialists to better insulate them from an ever more threatening environment. In order to do their jobs, these professionals must develop a deep understanding of their affluent clients. And, that understanding often identifies issues and concerns requiring your expertise.

As with executive coaches, there's a lot of chaff and little wheat. However, if you can find your way to the wheat, these family security consultants can be an exceptional source of new affluent clients. What you need to find are those personal security specialists who provide close protection or travel security or anti-stalking expertise to the wealthy. Most of these professionals tend to work with the exceptionally wealthy.

Because of their limited number, we had the opportunity to interview 22 family security consultants that work with the exceptionally wealthy, from celebrities to leading business people, and executives to the ultra-paranoid trust baby. What is clear is that:

- The family security consultants were looking to grow their businesses.

- They were not clear on the advantages of recommending a financial advisor to their affluent clients.

- They did not know how to make such a recommendation if the opportunity arose.

With the appropriate education, these issues evaporate leaving you with a steady stream of high-net-worth clients. By helping the family security consultants grow their business, by showing the benefit to them and their wealthy clients of referring you to those clients, and by teaching them how to bring you in, personal security specialists prove to be an untapped goldmine of affluent clients.

All in all, there is a wide variety of other professionals – other advisors to the affluent aside from private client attorneys and accountants – you can create strategic partnerships with. These other professionals – if you choose wisely and work the relationship properly – can result in a pipeline of new affluent clients. Some of the other types of professionals include:

- Corporate attorneys.

- Residential mortgage brokers.

- Hard-money lenders.

- Intellectual property attorneys.

- Appraisers.

- Medical practice executives.

- Executive search professionals.

- Third-party administrators.

- Morticians.

- Retirement community owners/managers.

- Commercial real estate brokers.

- Jet plane marketers.

- Hedge fund managers.

- Up-scale party planners.

- Jewelers.

- Family office executives.

- Real estate brokers.

- Art dealers.

- Private equity managers.

- Property and causalty insurance brokers.

- Credit-oriented bankers.

- Fundraisers.

- Investment bankers.

- Personal shoppers.

Conclusions

Let's review. You have a number of target markets for creating strategic partnerships – attorneys, traditional accountants, accountants who offer financial services and a wide variety of other professionals. All are good prospects, but each requires a different approach. Thus, you will have to customize your approach to capitalize on these opportunities.

Each type of professional may make some referrals now and again, and there is significant upside potential to establish a flow of clients. The power of this methodology lies in the finding that affluent clients follow the referral suggestions of their professional advisors most of the time – at least when we're dealing with accountants and private client attorneys. This means that if a professional makes a referral to you, your phone will ring. The challenge will be to significantly bump up the number of times this happens.

What you need to do is create a strategic partnership with these professionals. What you need is a proven process. And, that's what we detail in the next chapter.

Chapter 6

The Strategic Partnership Process

"The difference between a successful person and others is not a lack of strength, not a lack of knowledge, but rather a lack of will."
— Vince Lombardi

Up to this point, we have surveyed the private wealth market and concluded it is extremely large, certainly from the perspective of any individual financial advisor. It is also highly fragmented, which means that the structural advantage goes to the small, niche, competitor – the kind of competitor you are. We have also taken a good look at how the wealthy select financial advisors and we have zeroed in on the opportunity private client attorneys, accountants, and a few other professionals represent.

From this point forward, we will walk you through the complete process for creating that new affluent client pipeline. Simply put, the strategic partnership process consists of the following five steps (Exhibit 6.1):

- *The five strategic shifts*: the behavior observed in the Elite 1200 to become successful at building partnerships.

- *Foundational fundamentals*: required elements to concentrate on as you work the process.

- *Profiling your strategic partners*: understanding other professionals so you will know how to motivate them to refer their affluent clients to you.

- *Providing the economic glue*: how to deliver value and benefit on a consistent basis.

- *Keeping the pipeline full*: the discipline of ongoing implementation.

Exhibit 6.1: The Strategic Partnership Process

The Five Strategic Shifts

Focusing on the Basics

Profiling Strategic Partners

Providing Economic Glue

Keeping the Pipeline Full

Each of the next five chapters will discuss, in detail, each of the five steps in the strategic partnering process. But first, let's consider the predominant approaches financial advisors are employing today to motivate attorneys and accountants to provide them with referrals. Comparing our approach to that used by most advisors will show you the key differences.

The Predominant Approaches Financial Advisors Are Using Today

As we have seen, quite a few clients are already flowing from attorneys and accountants to advisors. A good many financial advisors are garnering new affluent clients from their relationships with accountants and attorneys. We find that many financial advisors are working hard to create what they call "strategic alliances." Therefore, we need to take a quick look at the way financial advisors are instituting these strategic alliances in order to better understand our concept of "strategic partnerships." But make this mental note now: they are very different in their overall impact to your bottom line.

The essential idea of a strategic alliance is when a financial advisor and an accountant (or attorney) believe they have a preferred role in working with one another. From the financial advisor's point of view, a strategic alliance means he or she will receive preferential treatment from the professional. There are many variations in the way financial advisors create and sustain strategic alliances; we have boiled these down into five predominant approaches (Exhibit 6.2):

- Communicating your money management process.

- Keeping "in front" of the professionals.

- Promoting new ideas, strategies, or products.

- Generating revenues for the professionals.

- Establishing formal joint-ventures.

Where the financial advisor "communicates his money management process" to accountants and/or attorneys. Erin works diligently to have at least one meeting a week with a qualified attorney or accountant. At these meetings, his goal is to clearly, concisely, and compellingly communicate the soundness of his money management process.

The financial advisor using this approach is attempting to differentiate himself through the quality of his money management processes, and hope that perhaps the attorney or accountant, so overwhelmed by this approach, will immediately offer up a client referral. However, the professionals have heard this many, many times before and, rather than differentiating, it serves the opposite function of putting the financial advisor in the faceless majority.

Where the financial advisor stays "in front" of accountants and/ or attorneys. Frank is a consummate networker. He's at every industry, community, and charity function. He's read the book, *"Never Eat Alone."* He goes all out making sure his breakfasts, lunches, and dinners are with accountants and attorneys. Periodically, Frank is provided with a referral from one of these professionals. However, these referrals are usually not very affluent.

The financial advisor adopting this approach is looking for (or creates) opportunities to talk to professionals. Taking the accountant to lunch or to a sporting event is quite common. By staying in contact, the financial advisor seeks to build a personal/professional relationship that will result in a wealthy client referral now and again.

Where the financial advisor briefs professionals on current ideas, strategies, and/or products. George is very technically proficient with respect to life insurance. He's aware of the latest trends and strategies. As new concepts and strategies come on his radar screen, he'll "run the circuit." This means George will contact every "center of influence" he has some (any) kind of relationship with and present the new concept or strategy. George is hoping that as he explains the strategy a light bulb will go off in the professional's head and that professional will have a client or two who would truly benefit from the strategy. This happens from time to time.

Where the financial advisor generates new business for the attorneys and/or accountants. Harry is very good about "trading" referrals. He keeps a sort of tally about which professionals he refers his affluent clients to and when he receives affluent client referrals in return. The problem is that Harry doesn't have enough wealthy clients needing either accounting or legal services to be able to build up his affluent clientele from the professionals he's working with.

In this variant, advisors make referrals to the professionals they know in the expectation that they will receive referrals in return. A big limitation of this approach is that financial advisors do not have sufficient clients to go one-for-one with all the professionals they seek to get referrals from. Another closely related variant is when financial advisors hire professionals directly, thereby generating new revenues for them.

In rarer instances, a financial advisor will create a formal partnership with a professional firm. We saw in a previous chapter that while many financial advisors have created formal partnerships with accounting firms, few of these relationships have borne fruit.

As noted, in this arrangement, the financial advisor has a formal contract or might even become an employee of the unit at the professional firm responsible for selling financial services. While this approach <u>can</u> prove to be profitable, more often it comes up short of expectations. It's not enough to get an agreement from the professional firm to do business together, there has to be a systematic process in place to get access to the wealthy continually (see *Chapter 11, Filling the Pipeline*).

Exhibit 6.2: What Financial Advisors are Generally Doing Today

Approaches	Actions
Your money management process	Present process during initial meetings
Keeping "in front" of the professionals	Social events; lunches
Promoting the new ideas, strategies or products	Often tax related; innovative products
Generating revenue for the professionals	Referrals; hiring them directly
Formal joint-venture	Firm-to-firm contract; becoming an employee of the professional firm

Many financial advisors use a combination of these approaches, tailored to their own strengths. These approaches, singly and in combination, do produce affluent client referrals, but they predominantly do so on an intermittent and infrequent basis. If your prospecting strategy with professionals is one or more of these four types, you will probably agree that you are not getting all the referrals you would like. Instead, it usually feels like you are knocking yourself out for not very much in return.

We do not recommend that you abandon these approaches. Instead, we suggest that you should merge them into a proven methodology and enhance your current efforts. That is, we propose that you use the approaches that are working for you today and make them part of a more systematic and productive process.

There are financial advisors who have already made this evolution. They have gone beyond these basic approaches and, through trial and error, made the way they garner affluent client referrals more systematic. They have created new affluent client pipelines for themselves. We know that the overwhelming majority of the Elite 1200 have significantly expanded beyond these basic approaches. In fact, we discovered the process we are describing to you by studying the habits of these highly successful financial advisors.

What we will NOT recommend is abandoning these basic approaches if you are currently using them – they work. Instead, what we advocate is selectively incorporating them into a broad-based professional relationship building process. These basic approaches can be used to create and deepen relationships with other professionals, and they do yield some referrals. However, these approaches do not create the free flowing pipeline of new wealthy clients that is our objective. Instead of a *strategic alliance*, the financial advisor has to evolve upwards and establish a *strategic partnership*.

If you're already working with accountants and attorneys, what we have found is that the process we'll be explaining is often best seen as an overlay on what you're already doing. In fact, the systematic process works best when it is used to augment the actions of financial advisors who presently have solid relationships with professionals.

Defining a Strategic Partnership

Many – but not all – financial advisors have "relationships" with accountants and/or attorneys, or the kind we have been calling *strategic alliances*. In general, high-quality relationships with these professionals will be <u>the optimal means</u> of obtaining new affluent clients – especially ultra-affluent clients. What we need to do is draw distinctions between the nature of the relationship most financial advisors have with these professionals – *strategic alliances* – and the type of relationship that results in the pipeline of new wealthy clients, what we term *strategic partnerships* (Exhibit 6.3).

With strategic alliances the financial advisor will usually get some client referrals. However, these referrals are generally sporadic. That is, every *once in a while* the accountant, for instance, will think of you and your services when considering a wealthy client situation. By contrast, in a strategic partnership, the accountant will be providing you with a consistent stream of wealthy clients needing your services and products, and properly prepped to talk with you.

Financial advisors who have strategic alliances are often one of a number of financial advisors that are doing business with the professional. For example, the attorney in a strategic alliance will be working with a number of financial advisors and will refer an affluent client to each of them from time to time. In a strategic partnership, you are the exclusive (or highly preferred) financial advisor and will receive the bulk of the referrals made by the professional.

As a strategic partner, the attorney or accountant is actively looking to make affluent client referrals to you. You facilitate this by implementing certain processes (see *Chapter 11, Filling the Pipeline*). The same cannot be said for strategic alliances, where the professional is not strongly motivated to make referrals to you.

Exhibit 6.3: A Comparison of Strategic Alliances and Strategic Partnerships

Strategic Alliances	Strategic Partnerships
Periodically an affluent client will be referred to you	On a regular basis, affluent clients are referred to you
You are one of a number of financial advisors referrals are made to	You are the only or primary financial advisor referrals are made to
The professional is not particularly looking to make a referral	The professional is actively looking to make a referral

When we tell advisors about these criteria, they say, if I was to go to an accountant and ask him for an exclusive, that accountant would say, "I'd love to give you an exclusive but I already have people I trade business with." If that's what you hear, that's fine. That's a strategic affiliation; however, it can be the start of a strategic partnership. But let's be perfectly clear, you can't build a strategic partnership by simply doing more of what got you an affiliation. What we want to do is show you how to bridge that gap, show you the changes the Elite 1200 made, and how you can make them.

Another point of distinction is that, in the case of strategic alliances, the financial advisors tend to have a number of professionals they are dealing with (Exhibit 6.4). For their part, financial advisors will generally report having an average of 15 to 20 such relationships, with some as high as 100 or even higher.

As we will see in the next chapter, when it comes to strategic partnerships we are basically talking about FIVE of them. There are many other professionals that you would be in contact with that will probably provide you with a wealthy client now and again. This we term the "bench." However, because of the time and effort you must commit to creating a pipeline of new affluent clients, we have found that FIVE is the optimal number of accountants and/or attorneys and/or other professionals most any financial advisor can establish strategic partnerships with.

Exhibit 6.4: Number of Strategic Alliances versus Number of Strategic Partnerships

Strategic Alliances   Strategic Partnerships

Another way of considering strategic partnerships is to examine some of their benefits for the financial advisor. In this comparison we will also include the situation where the financial advisor does not have any relationships with professionals.

Strategic partnerships generate the most and wealthiest referrals. This is because the advisor can adroitly focus on the accountant's or attorney's clientele in *strategic scenario sessions* (see *Chapter 11, Keeping the Pipeline Full*) and motivate the professional to refer (see *Chapter 10, The Economic Glue*). This will result in the financial advisor being able to get (on a relative basis) the greatest number of new wealthy clients. Moreover, these wealthy client referrals will be of high quality and will be pre-qualified. The result will be a significant financial return on effort for the financial advisor.

Conclusions

Creating and sustaining a pipeline of qualified, affluent clients does not happen overnight. It must be carefully constructed. Once constructed, it needs to be maintained. The process will take a lot of work, but the rewards are worth it.

It should be recognized by all parties that this process is neither quick nor simple. However, once mastered, it can lead to more affluent clients than any other methodology. This is perhaps why the Elite 1200, isn't the Elite 120,000.

In this chapter, we have just scratched the surface; we'll discuss each step in detail in its own chapter. We have outlined the process for creating that pipeline of new affluent clients. It starts with the way you must think about being a rainmaker. You then need to address the basics. You must understand the individual professional you're dealing with and be able to apply the economic glue. Finally, keeping the pipeline full entails the discipline of ongoing implementation.

It looks like a lot, but it's manageable. Like any new skill set, it gets easier with practice. The rewards of higher income and practice profitability will also be strong motivators for you to continue. Now, we turn our attention to how you need to think about what you're doing in order to create a pipeline of affluent clients from accountants and attorneys, as well as other types of professionals.

Chapter 7

The Five Strategic Shifts
of the Elite 1200

"Football is a game played with arms, legs and shoulders but mostly from the neck up."

– Knute Rockne

From the *traditional* "centers of influence" – accountants and attorneys – to other professionals such as executive coaches and personal security consultants, you have a tremendous opportunity to garner new affluent clients. The solution to having a steady stream of new wealthy clients wanting to do business with you is to create strategic partnerships with these professionals.

Bridging the gap from affiliations to partnerships is no small feat. In fact, it requires a strategic shift in thinking. The Elite 1200 often described this shift as having an "Aha" moment, or an epiphany, where suddenly it dawned on them how to approach this business.

Why did it take this epiphany to be successful? Because many of the principles of success to forge strategic partnerships run counter to common sense in that they go against the conventional, albeit inaccurate, information permeating the financial services industry. Only through years of trial and error, did the Elite 1200 navigate this path, which we'll now share with you.

The five strategic shifts are:

- The professional is the client.

- The end of referrals.

- The Law of Small Numbers.

- "You & I, Incorporated."

- The Economic Glue.

Let's now take a closer and more in-depth look at each of these strategic shifts.

The Professional is the Client

We run workshops for financial advisors on becoming a rainmaker – creating strategic partnerships with attorneys, accountants, and others. In all the workshops, we run the following exercise.

We ask the financial advisors in attendance: "Who is YOUR client?" If you're like most advisors, you may have paused a moment, then stated, "The accountant or attorney." We completely agree.

Take a moment and take a piece of paper and fold it in half. On one side put the initials of one of your better clients. On the other side, place the initials of a professional that has given you a referral in the last 18 months that you're working on getting a referral from, or, at a minimum, that you're aware of and has the potential to impact your business. Now answer the following questions for both your client and the professional:

- What are the names of their spouses?

- What are the names of their children and how old are they?

- Where did they go to college?

- What are the names of their pets?

- How do they make money?

- How much money do they average a year?

- How much money do they want to make per year?

- What are their interests outside of their jobs?

- What is their best and worst experience with a financial advisor?

If you're like most financial advisors, you'll see a pattern. Most financial advisors can do a very good job of answering these questions as they relate to their better clients. On the other hand, they seem to fall way short on answers when it comes to the professional. In effect, they're not treating the professional as a client. Therein lies the rub.

Intellectually, financial advisors readily acknowledge that the attorney or accountant is their client. However, the fact of the matter is this – the vast majority of financial advisors do not come close to the level of knowledge they have with their professional clients as they do with their better clients.

More painfully, the professionals have a much greater ability to impact the bottom line of any financial advisor than virtually any investor client. The first and most foundational step to becoming proficient at the RainMaker process is to begin to walk the talk on the fact that the attorney or accountant is your client.

Another indication of the gap in treating professionals as clients centers on their files. When we ask financial advisors in these workshops if they have files for their clients, everyone raises their hands. When we ask if they have files on the professionals they do business with, less than 1 in 30 raise their hands. So, open a file in your database on each of them, begin to populate it with the information you gather, and manage from that point of knowledge.

How can you translate this insight into action? First open and keep a file on them. If you have never met them before, we have found that many financial advisors find it useful to pre-qualify their professional prospects in some way, such as years in the business. Two common websites for this purpose are cpadirectory.com and martindale.com. We have also seen many financial advisors simply "Google" their prospects to both evaluate and learn about them. This step is also used to identify subjects for conversation as they prepare for their profiling meetings.

Profiling is obviously a skill you have developed over the course of your career with your clients. However, here we want to expand it a bit by engaging in a discovery process on the professional's business, learning such core things as their business model (the ways they make money), how they get their clients, what their clients look like, problems they are having with their clients, successes, failures, and goals. We will go into much more detail on this profiling process in the following chapter. Also, learn about them as a person. For example:

- Are they married, for how long, when is their anniversary?

- Do they have kids?

    ° How many?

    ° What are their names?

    ° What are their ages?

    ° Where are they going to school?

    ° What hobbies do they enjoy?

    ° What holidays do they see their kids?

- What interests do they have in life?

Once you find out this information, practice relationship management. In short, do all the things with the attorneys and accountants that you do with your best clients. Because that's exactly what they are – potentially your best clients. Remember, the professional advisors are the clients. They are never out of the loop. They're in the meetings they want to be in. You will often review your recommendations with them before presenting them to the affluent individual. In effect, you're working as a team, and they're usually the team leader. But as you get to know them, you'll develop a rhythm with how they like to work.

In a following chapter we discuss the Professional Profiling Tool. The information and insights you collect from this tool are the raw materials for your strategic partnerships.

The End of Referrals

Remember this statement for when it comes to growing your business through attorneys and accountants, as well as other types of professionals, "referral" is a destructive word. The word "referral" has a form of lingering mind pollution that causes financial advisors to misperceive the situation and destroy their partnerships, just as they're getting started.

Embedded in the definition of a referral is the idea that a client is being given to the financial advisor. This is precisely the case when a client is given to you (i.e., referred) by another client. They are handing this person over to a financial advisor. However, in the world of strategic partnerships, attorneys and accountants are not giving you a client. From their perspective, the individual remains their client. What they are doing is hiring you for a sleeve of products and services that they do not provide. In effect, you are a subcontractor.

There are two types of referrals:

- The "hand-off" referral is characteristic of a referral from a client. The client is saying: "I trust you, here's somebody, take care of them."

- The other type is what we call "Joint Venture Business" which is characteristic of what is received from an attorney or accountant. The professional is saying: "My client has a problem that I need your help with."

One advisor put this most poignantly with the following story. He said that prior to becoming a full-time financial advisor, he was an accountant for 15 years. In that time, he said he had given out literally hundreds of referrals. In all that time, with all those referrals, he said he had never gotten a call from the financial advisor, asking him his opinion of the product or service recommendation that was made to HIS client. Remember this fact, you are working as a team, and the attorney or accountant is the team leader, and it is your primary objective to make them look as good as possible. Communicate and work through the referring professional to their client. Over time, trust and rapport is established that allows this to become less rigid. But initially, it is imperative.

By avoiding this simple error of perception, in the eyes of an attorney or accountant, you will dramatically begin to separate yourself from the majority of financial advisors seeking the business from professionals. Of course, you must make sure your behavior follows in step with this insight.

The Law of Small Numbers

How many strategic partners do you need? As we've seen, on average, an attorney will refer a client with $2.7 million in assets in need of investment. Assuming a 1% payout, each client they refer will generate $27,000. That means you need to get four new clients to generate around $100,000 of additional annual revenue. And, most of these monies should end up going to the bottom line – income in your pocket.

The good news is you do not need a lot of strategic partners to significantly increase your income. In fact, the research on this point reveals a striking fact. The average number of partners for the Elite 1200 is 3.9.

Perhaps even more interesting, it never goes above five. In fact, when advisors tried to work with more than five, their production began to go down. Why? It appears that they could not "feed" all of these strategic partnerships adequately, and began to backslide into affiliations as opposed to partnerships.

As a function of the Law of Small Numbers, in finding your strategic partners, we have the concept of N.E.X.T. Finding strategic partners is not about selling them on you. Rather it is about finding someone with whom you click that has the ability and willingness to impact your business. Strategic partnerships are marriages; they are not dates. You need someone with whom you get along very well. Only by finding the right strategic partners will you be able to join the ranks of the Elite 1200. To aid you in this process, it is not important, but rather critical, that you keep a simple word at hand. That word is N.E.X.T.

N.E.X.T. stands for: **Never Expend X-tra Time**.

Our experience with financial advisors is replete with what have been characterized as good working relationships that had gone on for years. They usually consisted of the financial advisor taking a professional to lunch three times a year and never receiving a single opportunity for joint venture business. If you're not getting new affluent clients after a reasonable amount of time, use the word: N.E.X.T.

For example, in one workshop, we had a financial advisor approach us after the meeting to ask our advice on a situation with an accountant. He said that he knew an accountant that had some very wealthy clients but he could not get any referrals from him. We asked him to tell us about his relationship. He said they had known each other for three years, and in that time he had given a lot of referrals from his clientele to the accountant but had yet to receive any referrals in return. Whenever he'd ask the accountant if he had any referrals, the accountant would ask him, "What is it that you do exactly?" We asked him how many referrals he had given to the accountant, and he thought for a moment, and said, "35." It is easy to leap to the conclusion that this person was just foolish. However, in our experience it is unfortunately quite common – in occurrence, if not degree. Too many financial advisors persist in the idea that if they could just get Attorney X or Accountant Y to make a referral, they'd be on their way. But remember this critical idea. If it is not happening, say, "N.E.X.T." and move on.

After being trained on our profiling process, this advisor uncovered the fact that this accountant had a relative that was a financial advisor who received all of his referrals. The unlucky financial advisor had wasted three years and 35 referrals, because he neglected to evaluate the accountant's ability to send referrals back. We are not looking to establish friendships, but rather business partnerships.

While we advocate moving on when a professional will not become a strategic partner, you nevertheless must be as careful not to use N.E.X.T. too quickly. To aid you in this process we have a N.E.X.T. Litmus Test:

- Do you have a good relationship personally?

- Does the professional have the ability to refer, and the wealth level you seek?

- Does the advisor want to make money?

- Do you have a possible joint business arrangement?

If you answered "NO" to any one of these questions, it may be time to say N.E.X.T. Remember this thought: *You are choosing them; they are not choosing you*. If your potential strategic partners don't meet these criteria, chances are they aren't going to help you join the ranks of the Elite 1200 either.

We've found that it's very hard for financial advisors to say N.E.X.T. Ira was "close" with an accountant who had a stellar clientele. While the accountant had only about 60 clients, half of those clients had a net worth of $20 million or more. As Ira would say it, he's been cultivating this accountant since the fifth grade when they lived on the same block in the Bronx.

After profiling the accountant (see *Chapter 9, The Professional Profiling Tool*), Ira discovered that the accountant *only* believes in indexing. Ira, on the other hand, is a big advocate of professional money managers. Ira should be saying N.E.X.T. Instead, he's confident that he can convince the accountant of the value of professional money management. It's very unlikely to happen.

We see examples over and over again where financial advisors should, but do not, say N.E.X.T. Another financial advisor, after profiling a professional he was "working on" for years, said it would probably be a good idea to cross the attorney off his list, but he already put so much time and effort in, he just wanted to try for a little while longer. After we looked at his profile of this attorney, we readily concluded that N.E.X.T. would be the only rational response. This is like seeing a stock lose value and you know it's going to continue to lose value but somehow you're hoping it will turn around. It won't.

Whether it's because of the allure of a professional's clientele or because a financial advisor spent so much time cultivating a professional, many have a very difficult time saying N.E.X.T. You must be able to say N.E.X.T.

"You & I, Incorporated"

The big picture, critical issue in building a "You & I, Inc." is to shift from a sales approach to a marketing approach. Ask yourself, what is the fundamental difference between these two disciplines of Sales versus Marketing? In one of our workshops, one clever financial advisor quipped, "Getting Paid." While amusing, this is exactly the kind of thinking that can prevent you from building a partnership – expecting a return too quickly.

The classic definition of "Sales" is selling what you have. The classic definition of "Marketing" is finding out the prospect's needs and wants first and selling to those needs and wants second. Fundamentally, this section is about a shift from a sales approach to a marketing approach. While that may seem "too obvious," it is the simple, but fundamental, change that allows you to achieve two critical goals with any attorney or accountant:

- Differentiation.

- Value.

To get us started, it helps to put yourself in the shoes of an accountant or an attorney, and see what it is like for them as they are pursued by financial advisors seeking referrals.

Exhibit 7.1: New Financial Advisors Visiting Attorneys and Accountants

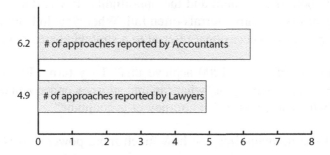

N = 619 private client lawyers; 251 accountants

Source: The Private Client Lawyer (Wealth Management Press, 2003); Prince & Associates, 2004.

Attorneys and accountants are regularly besieged by financial advisors wanting their clients. In fact, attorneys receive an average of 4.9 visits from new financial advisors every six months. Accountants receive an average of 6.2 visits every six months. This is usually the start and the finish; in other words, the dead-end of the whole process. Why? Because financial advisors come by month after month saying essentially the same thing, such as: "I manage money, do you have any referrals?"

Think about that. If you go in with that message, as far as the attorneys or accountants are concerned, you have just become a member of a long, monotonous, and undifferentiated parade through their offices. Accordingly, the encounter inevitably concludes with vague allusions of reciprocal referrals, give a client to get a client.

Due to this less than enthusiastic reception, the response of financial advisors is to see more and hope they connect. They play a numbers game: "If I see more professionals, I'll get more referrals." But in the world of strategic partnerships, a numbers game is a loser's game. To succeed, you need to go deeper, not broader.

How do lawyers and accountants react to this onslaught of contacts? Typically, they are polite but unresponsive, and often impatient and annoyed. Their thought process is here comes another one that wants access to my clients, but doesn't know the first thing about my business or about me.

Listen very carefully to these words, knowing the professional's business is both the problem and the opportunity. If you don't know it, that's why efforts to gain referrals often fail. When you do learn it, that's why they go from an occasional referral to a strategic partnership.

So how do the Elite 1200 achieve this? They turn 180 degrees in strategy. From a mentality of "what can that attorney or accountant do for me?" to "what can I do for that attorney or accountant?"

Just for a moment, imagine how much more powerful it is to have someone approach you that genuinely is interested in getting to know you, your business, your business model, how you make your living, your successes, your failures, what problems you are having, and how they can help you. Even proactively bringing ideas to the table to solve your problems or help you achieve your goals. Compare this to taking you out to lunch and in turn wanting a much bigger favor, an affluent client referral? That's exactly what we are talking about here. It's what one of the Elite 1200 described in a very compelling way, he called it building a "You & I, Incorporated."

The Elite 1200 are very adept at forging these relationships for a couple of reasons. First they possess the important basics. In other words, they are technically competent as it relates to products and services and exhibit a high degree of integrity. These are absolutely necessary to demonstrate to an attorney or accountant. But in analyzing the behavior of the Elite 1200, they do three important things to achieve a "You & I, Inc." Partnership. Here's the three steps:

1) Build rapport;

2) Evaluate potential; and

3) Hunt for a way to add value.

Interestingly, the majority of financial advisors begin at the same point – build rapport – but they also stop there. By using the professional profiling tool, you're shifting gears (see *Chapter 9, The Professional Profiling Tool*). It's no longer about you and what you do. Instead, it's about the professionals and what their worlds are all about.

The Economic Glue of Strategic Partnerships

There are two ways you can provide value to professionals – we refer to them as direct and indirect financial incentives.

Direct financial incentives fall into one of three categories:

• Revenue sharing in product sales.

• Generating professional fees.

• Reciprocal referrals.

For those professional who are licensed and able to split commissions and fees, then you're going to go that way. Why not? The simplest transaction is the best. However, there's a serious problem with this approach. The vast majority of your target partners don't do this, or don't want to do this (see *Chapter 5, Accountants and Attorneys as Strategic Partners*).

What about generating professional fees? If you or a client has a real need for legal or accounting services, this is always welcome. However, it rarely amounts to the kind of perceived value that can be the foundation of a strategic partnership, because the fees are just too small.

What about trading clients? Many affiliations are about "trading" business – you refer clients to them and they refer some of their clients to you. As we noted, there are many limitations inherent in this approach. Specifically, you cannot possibly provide enough clients to accountants and attorneys to get enough clients back to ensure your spot in the Elite 1200. It's just that trading clients is for nearly every financial advisor a mathematical impossibility.

This is especially the case when we consider other types of professionals. If you seek to partner with a divorce attorney, for example, it's simply not possible to say to one of your clients: "Now that your financial plan is up to date, how's your marriage because I know a great divorce attorney..."

So what do the Elite 1200 do? It turns out that they strongly focus on indirect financial incentives as opposed to direct financial incentives. Therefore, what we're going to focus on is indirect financial incentives. In profiling the professional advisor, you'll find that they'll pretty much tell you ways you can provide indirect financial incentives (see *Chapter 10, The Economic Glue*).

Conclusions

If you want to become one of the Elite 1200, you're going to have to have a book of wealthy clients. The optimal prospecting approach is to access these affluent clients from "centers of influence" – especially accountants and attorneys. In order to be successful in this regard, you'll need to approach the matter with a particular mindset.

The five strategic shifts we've discussed in this chapter encompass the way you have to think about building strategic partnerships. Nearly all the financial advisors in our workshops, as well as the very high-end financial advisors we individually coach, have needed to make these five strategic shifts.

Experience has also taught us that this is the hardest part of the strategic partnership process. Once you have incorporated these five strategic shifts into your thinking and practice, becoming adept at the rest of the process tends to be quite intellectually easy.

No matter what professional you're sourcing wealthy clients from, you have to be attentive to the basics. In the next chapter, we address these basics.

Chapter 8

Foundational Fundamentals

"Before you can win, you have to believe you are worthy."
– Mike Ditka

We agree on the importance of attorneys and accountants as sources of new affluent clients for financial advisors like you. Further, we have established that affluent clients depend on the advice of their attorneys and accountants so they usually follow through with these referrals. We have also provided an overview describing what most financial advisors are doing to build relationships with these professionals, as well as an overview of the steps involved in strategic partnerships. In the previous chapter, we addressed the way you have to think about and approach this type of business in order to succeed – the five strategic shifts.

Throughout this book, we have emphasized that this process of creating a pipeline of new affluent clients is robust. It is reliable and effective. That is why it is the process perfected and used by the Elite 1200 – the million dollar income financial advisors. At the same time, when we look at all the research, we find there are a number of expectations accountants and attorneys have of financial advisors. These are the elements these types of professionals seek from financial advisors looking to enlist them as strategic partners.

Please note: Although we will recommend specific actions, keep in mind that everything should be customized to the professional you are creating a relationship with, which is why the following chapter is at the core of the strategic partnering process (see *Chapter 9, The Professional Profiling Tool*).

Our discussion of the "basics" is predicated on research conducted with hundreds of attorneys and accountants. These multi-year research projects have generated the empirically-derived insights we are sharing with you. In addition, our views have been refined by years of coaching and consulting work in assisting members of the Elite 1200 build strategic partnerships with professionals. We have also implemented this program with fast-tracking financial advisors who are quickly moving to elite status. In this chapter we will discuss:

- *The Basics* – the importance and role of personal integrity and technical expertise.

- *Personal Integrity* – what it is and how to communicate it.

- *Personal Integrity and Being a Team Player* – the reassurance accountants and attorneys are looking for.

- *Personal Integrity and Avoiding the "Edge"* – staying well clear of gray areas.

- *Technical Expertise* – don't assume your strategic partners know what you know.

The Basics

When you build a house, you start with the foundation. When you build a relationship, you have to attend to the foundational elements as well. A strategic partnership is a relationship, and building it right, from the foundation up, requires time and thought. The two basics are:

- Personal integrity.

- Technical expertise.

Think about it. Lawyers and accountants will simply not refer their wealthy clients to financial advisors who do not have personal integrity and who are not technically competent. Therefore, it falls to you to show that you are abundantly well qualified in both areas.

In RainMaker workshops, we've yet to find financial advisors who profess to be cheats, con artists, or incompetents (a lack of technical expertise). While we refer to these "basics" as universally important, *how* you communicate and work through them is up to you and depends on your evaluation of your strategic partner. It's a mistake many financial advisors make to presume that, in working with "centers of influence," these professionals will "see' that you have personal integrity and that you're technically proficient. Unless you're able to adroitly communicate your abilities with respect to these areas, you're unlikely to get the chance to work with their wealthy clients.

If you are not able to meet these requirements in the eyes of your strategic partner, then you are unlikely to ever again see a referral from them – affluent or otherwise. Understanding these basics is essential for financial advisors in order to work effectively with accountants and attorneys. Let's now explore the issue of personal integrity in greater detail.

Personal Integrity

When we talk about the basics, we need to start with the most important one – personal integrity. Working collaboratively between professionals and financial advisors on wealthy client situations calls for tremendous levels of personal integrity and trust. It is impossible to foresee all the situations and ramifications that will arise and negotiate them in advance. All the experts involved must therefore trust each other, and such trust is the byproduct of integrity. Indeed, personal integrity is deemed to be essential by virtually all of the attorneys (98.4%) and accountants (99.2%) we surveyed (Exhibit 8.1).

Exhibit 8.1: Importance of Personal Integrity

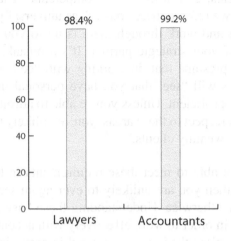

N = 619 private client lawyers; 251 accountants

Source: Creating a Pipeline of New Affluent Clients (2003).

How can you be sure the attorney or accountant you are working with is convinced of your personal integrity? You communicate your views and values to them. It is important for financial advisors to communicate their perspectives in ethical standards to attorneys and accountants. Among attorneys and accountants, the financial advisors who do go out of their way to discuss ethical and professional standards are seen as having a high degree of personal integrity.

As you plan your discussion points, you should reflect on the fact that personal integrity has two facets. One facet is how the financial advisor will deal with the professionals who refer their affluent clients. What the professionals are looking for is a team player; they want the financial advisor to show that he or she is on the professional's team.

The other facet of personal integrity is the extent to which the financial advisor will do right by the wealthy client. These days, attorneys and accountants will shun financial advisors who go "over the edge" to profit. In recent years, financial advisors have been known to promote strategies and products that are well into the gray area of legality, uncomfortably so for many professionals. Some of these strategies and products end up not being red flagged by the professional because the financial advisor has directed the wealthy client to a more accommodating professional. This is considered a huge breach of trust by the professional. Above all, the professional needs the financial advisor to be a team player.

Personal Integrity and Being a Team Player

One of the most important aspects of personal integrity is being a team player in all the ways the professional wants you to be. The attorney or accountant who is orchestrating the engagement wants to be confident that everything client-related is progressing in an appropriate and thoughtful manner. They need to ensure that things are going well for their wealthy client, and the easiest way to do this is to work with a financial advisor who understands that serving the affluent client is a team effort and the professional is captain of the team. After all, the accountant or attorney relies on that client coming back to them in the future for more work. In the mind of the professional, all referrals they are making to financial advisors fall into the category of "joint-business" (see *Chapter 7, The Five Strategic Shifts*).

However, that is not the situation today. There are many failures of collaboration between attorneys and accountants with financial advisors. Sometimes, the professionals failed to make certain that they guided the process with the affluent client, other times the financial advisor cut the professional out of the loop. In fact, almost EVERY attorney (95.2%) and accountant (94.4%) reported having lost control of the process to financial advisors at least once over the previous three-year period (Exhibit 8.2). Think about that; is it any wonder they have sensitivity on this issue? Losing control of the affluent client creates a serious breach with the professional, and will certainly mean a cessation of all referrals.

Exhibit 8.2: Losing Control of the Process

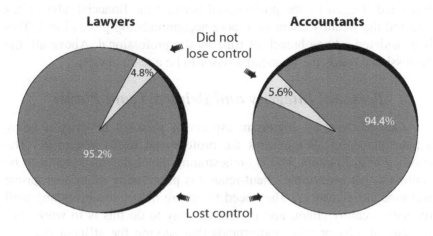

N = 619 private client lawyers; 251 accountants

Source: Creating a Pipeline of New Affluent Clients (2003).

Lawyers and accountants want to stay involved with their clients, even after they have referred them to you. They also need financial advisors to clearly understand their role (Exhibit 8.3). It is the rare attorney (6.0%) or accountant (5.2%) who does not have a story (or two or three) about financial advisors who have overstepped their bounds.

Often, problems emerge because the financial advisor receiving the referral has not gone to the trouble of making sure that the professional's communication needs are being met. Often, the professional and the financial advisor make different assumptions about the division of responsibilities between them. Usually the professional assumes they will be kept in the loop, and the financial advisor assumes that they do not need to be consulted. In these situations, the result is that wealthy clients are not as well served as they might be. Not only that, the relationship between the financial advisor and the attorney or accountant is severely damaged. These poor outcomes can often be avoided if there is better communication.

**Exhibit 8.3: Importance of Referred Financial Advisors
Understanding Their Roles**

N = 619 private client lawyers; 251 accountants

Source: Creating a Pipeline of New Affluent Clients (2003).

Personal integrity means more than just good communications. It also refers to what you will, and will not do, with and for the wealthy client.

Personal Integrity and Avoiding the "Edge"

Personal integrity also entails doing right by the wealthy client. "Doing right" by a client is a relative concept. You will have to figure out where your boundaries are, and be prepared to share them with your professional strategic partners. At a minimum, this means not promoting strategies or products that will create problems for the wealthy client later on.

There are quite a number of financial advisors, for instance, who have gone too far when it comes to working the tax situation of an affluent client. Abusive tax schemes fall into this category. Abusive trust schemes usually entail the creation of a number of trusts (either domestic or offshore) to which the client assigns selected assets and income. The trusts are vertically layered so that each trust distributes income to the next trust. Bogus expenses are charged against the trust income, thereby reducing the taxable income. At the same time, the illusion of separation and control is created. Although the financial advisor is officially the trustee, the affluent client actually still controls the trust.

There are quite a number of abusive domestic trust arrangements, including:

- *The abusive asset management company.* An asset management company formed as a domestic trust is created where the affluent client is the director and the financial advisor or professional is the trustee responsible for running the asset management company. The objective of this arrangement is for the client to convey the impression that he or she is not managing his or her businesses, thereby starting the layering process.

- *The abusive business trust.* The affluent client transfers a business to a trust, receiving certificates or units of beneficial interest. The business trust makes payments to the unit holders – the client – or to other trusts, so that the business trust does not have to pay any taxes. The business trust can be set up such that the units are canceled at death or sold to the owner's heirs for a nominal cost, thus avoiding estate taxes.

- *The abusive family residence trust.* The affluent client transfers his or her family residence (including furnishings) to a trust, receiving units that are claimed to be part of a taxable exchange. The exchange results in a stepped-up basis for the property. At the same time, the owner does not report a gain. The trust is thus in the rental business and claims to rent the residence back to the affluent client. However, in many instances, no rent is paid as the owner and family are identified as caretakers of the property.

- *The abusive final trust.* When a number of abusive trusts are being employed, some affluent clients create a final trust that holds the trust units of other abusive trusts and is the distributor of their income. Commonly, the final trust is created in a foreign jurisdiction that imposes little, if any, tax on the trust.

There are many points of view on ethical standards and what constitutes personal integrity. You have your bottom line, and you will want to create long-term, mutually profitable relationships with people who share your perspective. If you and the professionals you are working with do not share the same sense of personal integrity, it is unlikely that a strategic partnership can be created.

For ethical as well as fiduciary reasons, professionals are only interested in working with (and referring their wealthy clients to) financial advisors who they believe share their sense of personal integrity. Personal integrity is one of the two "basic" foundation elements of a strategic partnership. The other basic element is technical expertise. For obvious reasons, professionals are only willing to work with, and refer their affluent clients to, financial advisors who are knowledgeable and competent.

Technical Expertise

Like personal integrity, technical expertise is absolutely "basic." Not surprisingly, accountants and attorneys weigh technical expertise highly in deciding whom to work with. These professionals make technical expertise a top criterion in choosing the financial advisors they will ask to help serve their high-net-worth clients. Technical expertise is essential when it comes to selecting financial advisors who are highly skilled in their specialty (Exhibit 8.4).

Exhibit 8.4: Importance of Technical Expertise

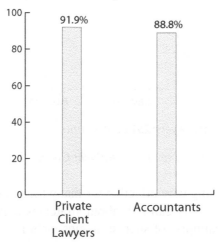

N = 619 private client lawyers; 251 accountants

Source: Creating a Pipeline of New Affluent Clients (2003).

There are several ways to communicate technical expertise. One is simply to raise technical issues for discussion. It's important for financial advisors to open and maintain a dialog on technical expertise with accountants and attorneys. In this way, they can get a better handle on the technical competencies of their strategic partners, and be in a better position to know where they can add value.

Another way to demonstrate technical expertise is to convey new client solutions. Lawyers and accountants are under significant competitive pressure and the world of private client work is especially fast-moving. As a result, 75.3% of the attorneys and 82.1% of the accountants said they were looking for state-of-the-art strategies and product ideas (Exhibit 8.5). Financial advisors seeking strategic partnerships can add considerable value by bringing new strategies and product ideas to these professionals.

Exhibit 8.5: Looking for State-of-the-Art Strategies and Product Ideas

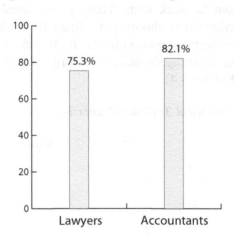

N = 619 private client lawyers; 251 accountants

Source: Creating a Pipeline of New Affluent Clients (2003).

What is proving very effective for many financial advisors using this approach is when they can talk about strategies being employed by the ultra-affluent. Examples of such strategies include:

- A family office was able to "lock in" their executive director as an employee for a set number of years and ensure monies would be available to source a replacement if that person died or became disabled. What makes this strategy so attractive to the family office is that they are managing the monies that will be used to pay out in case of disaster or as a form of deferred compensation. Moreover, the monies set aside for this purpose grow in a tax-free environment.

- An ultra-affluent family used special purpose entities to provide asset protection for a number of family businesses as well as a way to obtain credit at exceptionally low interest rates. The loans are then used to fund a series of entities used for estate planning enabling selected family members to get a tax-advantaged revenue stream potentially in perpetuity. Meanwhile, nearly all the income taxes owed by the family were offset by the interest payments on the loans.

- Another strategy enables the wealthy to convert taxable income such as that generated by investing in hedge funds into monies that are taxed as either dividends or capital gains or – in some cases – not at all as opposed to being taxed as ordinary income. Clearly, this can result in a meaningful increase in return on a hedge fund investment. As noted, these tax benefits are the by-product of providing the ultra-affluent a way to better manage certain personal and/or business risks.

- One ultra-affluent family transferred a majority of their operating business assets as well as their commercial and personal real estate into an offshore structure. They then reconfigured the assets and "hedged them." This placed all the assets outside the reach of creditors, yet still available for use by the family. Moreover, the strategy enabled the near tax-free inter-family transfer of assets at a discounted rate of 68%.

- As various countries have meaningfully different tax codes, a goodly number of the ultra-affluent engage in tax-arbitrage among these jurisdictions. A variety of strategies exist that permit the wealthy with multiple business interests to facilitate the efficacious use of capital as well as offset currency risks. This is akin to corporate transfer pricing. As a by-product, the

personal taxes they would have otherwise had to pay are miti-
gated or eliminated.

- One ultra-affluent family discounted the value of their fine art
  and numismatic collection using a leveraged derivative transaction. These collectibles will eventually be transferred to the
  next generation at – what they project to be – one-fifteenth their
  current market value because of the tax savings due to the accu-
  mulated interest on the loans, as well as from the discounting
  process.

- An affluent celebrity was able to create a deferred compensation plan using an offshore structure. The entity was paid all
  monies earned by the celebrity outside the United States. All
  the monies in the offshore structure are disclosed to the IRS.
  Still, all estate and gift taxes on these funds have been negated.
  The matter of income with respect to decedent is likewise
  abrogated. Monies that will eventually come out of the entity
  are taxed at 15% or less. Also, in the case that the celebrity's
  investment in artistic projects lose money, he will be reim-
  bursed those funds from the entity on a tax-free basis. Finally,
  the funds in the offshore structure grow tax-deferred.

While the implementation of these strategies for the wealthy require
a very specific fact pattern, your ability to intelligently discuss them
regularly conveys a high level of technical expertise to accountants and
attorneys. Moreover, you need not be the authority, but if you can bring
in such an expert who is part of your operation, then you'll achieve the
same results.

Another way financial advisors can demonstrate technical expertise
is by responding to changes in the regulatory environment. An effective
approach to communicating technical expertise is assisting accountants
and attorneys in managing affluent client situations that have significantly changed due to external factors. Typically, these events are a function
of regulatory and tax law changes. Financial advisors have an opportunity
to enhance their strategic partnerships by being proactive in informing the
professionals they are working with.

Conclusions

Professional relationships, like personal ones, have to be built on trust and sustained through interaction. Trust is established when people feel that they can count on each other in important ways. Between a financial advisor and a professional, trust is created when the professional trusts the financial advisor not to endanger an affluent client's interest or to jeopardize the relationship between the client and the professional. Trust is enhanced further as a financial advisor helps the client-professional bond become stronger.

Professionals need to know two things about an advisor in order to trust them. They need to know about the <u>integrity</u> of the financial advisor, and whether or not their ethical standards coincide. The bond between wealthy client and professional is built on integrity, and so is the bond between professional and financial advisor.

The other thing they need to know about a financial advisor in order to trust them is their <u>technical expertise</u>. Clients trust their professionals and financial advisors to be technical experts, and technical expertise is an essential part of the value provided to high-net-worth clients. Technical expertise is one of the areas in which a professional truly values a financial advisor.

The key to becoming a rainmaker is by first mastering the basics. Herein, the basics are professional integrity and technical expertise.

While, conceptually, the basics are across the board essential, what they mean for any particular professional is likely to vary. So, customization is essential. Furthermore, we've emphasized the need for considerable customization all along. The way you'll know how to customize your approach – including how to add value – is by developing a deep understanding of each professional you work with. And, the way to develop such an understanding is the professional profiling tool.

Chapter 9

The Professional Profiling Tool

"It is a fine thing to have ability, but the ability to discover ability in others is the true test."

– Lou Holtz

Have you ever walked up to a new affluent client, looked them up and down, and said: "You need 50% of your portfolio in international small cap." How about looked into a wealthy client's eyes (the mirror of the soul and all that) and said: "You need $5 million of second-to-die. I can feel it."

In order to make recommendations to wealthy clients, you need to understand what is important to them, what they have, what they want to accomplish, and so forth. Furthermore, the client needs to understand that you understand. The same logic holds true when working with accountants and attorneys.

What we've found central to the success of financial advisors who want to create a steady stream of new affluent clients is their insight into the lives and worlds of their strategic partners. As we said initially, this process is not about new paradigms or thinking outside the box. On the contrary, it's about leveraging and redirecting what you already do well – no doubt, quite well. What we're doing here is taking your ability to profile your wealthy clients and applying these same interpersonal skills to working with professionals.

What we've found is that most financial advisors, once they understand what they need to do, lack a methodology for collecting and organizing this information about the "centers of influence" they're proposing to establish strategic partnerships with. In evaluating the Elite 1200, we identified the foundation for this methodology, and in coaching other financial advisors refined it. The result is the professional profiling tool.

The Tool

You start filling out the professional profiling tool by noting what you know about a particular accountant or attorney or any other professional you believe might make a good strategic partner. It is advisable to verify your understanding of the professional using the second approach to gathering information – ask them.

As we said, this approach is not much different than what you do when working with an affluent client, albeit expanded a bit. In order to develop a detailed profile of the accountant or attorney or any other type of professional you are evaluating as a strategic partner, the following nine areas are often essential:

1. The professionals as people.

2. Their goals and objectives for their practice.

3. Their perspective on various financial services and products.

4. How they are managing their practices.

5. Their current clientele.

6. The marketing approaches they employ.

7. How they are compensated and how this is impacting their lives.

8. Their relationships with financial advisors.

9. Their openness and willingness to working with you.

Let's look at each of these areas, including the rationale behind each one, as well as sample questions. What you must be very clear about is that it is not the specific questions that are important but the kind of information you need to solicit. You need to gain a thorough appreciation of the professional's particular – if not idiosyncratic – life and world.

The Person

You are looking to determine the professionals' histories and motivations, as well as their evolution in their practice. You are also interested in them as people in order to establish and maintain rapport.

Sample questions:

- How did you get into this business?

- How long have you been at the firm?

- What is your area of expertise?

  ° Why did you decide to specialize in this area?

- What do you enjoy most about your work?

- What other accounting firms (or law firms) have you been a part of?

- What designations or certifications do you hold?

- Ideally, where would you like to be when you are 45? 55? 65? 75?

- If you did not have to work anymore, what would you do?

- What area of practice were you most interested in during school?

- How long have you and your wife been married?

- How old are your children?

  ° Are they married, in college, play sports, etc.?

- Do you have grandchildren?

- What do you do to relax?

    ○   What are your hobbies?

Practice Goals and Objectives

What you are looking for are accountants, attorneys, and other professionals who are motivated to be more financially successful or are seeking to enhance their lifestyles without giving up income. In effect, you are trying to ascertain if the professional you are talking to will respond to the added value you will be providing.

Sample questions:

- How would you describe your role?

- What is your specialty?

- What are the goals and objectives for your practice?

    ○   How important is it to you to build your practice and earn more?

    ○   Where do you see your practice in five years? Ten years?

    ○   How do you see the profits of your practice growing?

- How do you see your client base growing?

    ○   Number of clients.

    ○   Net worth of clients.

- How important is it to you to work less but maintain your current income?

- How much free time do you see next year?

- How much pro-bono work do you do?

- How long do you plan on practicing law (accounting)?

  ○ When do you expect to retire?

- Is there someone at the firm who will eventually succeed you?

- How do you benefit from referring your clients to other professionals in your firm?

- If we were sitting here three years from today, what would have had to have happened to make you happy with your practice?

Financial Product Issues

You need to determine their knowledge and comfort with the financial products you provide. This is most easily seen with respect to life insurance. Say, the attorney or accountant is not life insurance friendly. That is, they strongly believe in buying term and investing the rest. If you are a financial advisor focusing on selling life insurance, then a professional with this point of view is highly unlikely to be a good candidate as a strategic partner. With respect to that professional, you should say N.E.X.T.

Sample questions:

- What is the role of life insurance in the planning you do for your clients?

  ○ How do you feel about life insurance as a planning tool?

  ○ Do you feel life insurance is overused or underused in estate planning?

  ○ How familiar are you with the various forms of life insurance and how they can be used?

- What are your thoughts on managed money?

- How much life insurance do you have?

- How do you manage your own money?

- How aware are you of the various state-of-the-art investment strategies?

- When was the last time a client asked you about investments?

    ○ How did you answer it?

Practice Management

In order to help your potential strategic partners become more successful you have to understand how they manage their practices today. This covers a very broad range of concerns and factors from their current revenue model to the processes they use to work with their wealthy clients. By understanding their practices, you will also be able to adapt the way you work with affluent clients in their approach to the matter.

Sample questions:

- How do you build your practice?

- What is the main focus of your practice?

- What percentage of your practice is "trusts and estates" plans?

    ○ What percentage of your income is "trusts and estates" planning?

- How do you present ideas and issues to your clients?

- What is your work process?

    ○ What is your follow-up "system"?

- Do you do financial modeling?

- Are you happy with the way your firm works?

- Are you part of a study group?

- How do you allocate profits at your firm?

- How do you illustrate a financial issue or plan to your clients?

  ° Computer printout, executive summary, verbally, yellow pad?

- Do your clients usually follow your recommendations?

- How often do you contact your clients either by phone or in person?

  ° What about your 10 best clients?

- How do you keep current on tax law changes?

- How interested are you in learning about new planning strategies and concepts?

- If estate taxes were repealed, how would this affect your practice?

  ° What would you do?

- What is the partners/associates ratio?

  ° Staffing breakdown in your practice...firm?

- Do you set and practice goals?

- Are you part of the management team?

- How many different practice areas are at your firm?

- How many billable hours are expected of you?

  ° From your associates?

- What does your typical workweek look like?

    ◦ How many client meetings?

- How many hours per week do you usually put in?

- Would you act as a trustee?

The Professional's Clientele

In order to leverage the current client base of the accountant or attorney, you have to know what it looks like. We have found that many, if not most, financial advisors have an often overly optimistic view of the number and wealth and needs of the clienteles of the professionals they are dealing with. It is necessary to clearly understand the professional's clientele, for this will provide you with an accurate financial assessment of the potential pipeline.

Sample questions:

- How many clients do you have?

    ◦ What does having a client entail?

- What markets are you in?

    ◦ Do you work with many business owners, executives, retirees, physicians...?

- What does your "typical" client look like?

    ◦ Net worth.

    ◦ Age.

    ◦ Geographic location.

    ◦ Income.

    ◦ Marital status.

- How did you meet your best client?

- What percentage of your clientele is charitably inclined?

    ° Describe values of a typical client.

    ° What are examples of things they are doing?

    ° Are any of them on the boards of charities?

- How many of your clients are C-corporations?

- Do you specialize in any specific industry?

- Do you have a client rating system?

- Do you do automatic reviews?

    ° How often?

- What are average fees per client per year?

Marketing

There is usually a tremendous amount of value-added you can provide accountants and attorneys when it comes to helping them acquire new wealthy clients. What we have found is that this is one of the strongest forms of economic glue there is. However, in order to add value, you have to first understand what they are doing today, as well as how effective these actions are.

Sample questions:

- How many new clients do you usually get in a year?

    ° How many new clients do you want to add this year?

- How do you get new clients?

    ° Referrals from attorneys, referrals from accountants, referrals from financial advisors, client referrals, seminars, public relations activities, and so forth.

    ° (If referrals from another advisor) Where do you get your new clients from?

    ° Why do you think this marketing approach works for you?

- Who are your competitors?

- Do you have a Marketing Director at your firm?

- Do you have a marketing plan?

- Do you use outside marketing advisors?

- What is the image of your firm?

- What are your practice goals for new business?

- Membership to local civic, charitable, professional organizations?

- What are your thoughts on multidisciplinary practices?

- What is the firm's viewpoint concerning business development?

- Do you run seminars?

    ° What kind?

    ° What have been the most successful seminars for you?

    ° Do you have seminars for prospects? Advisors?

Compensation

This issue cuts to the essence of the matter of economic glue. The overwhelming percentage of accountants and attorneys are looking for ways to boost their incomes. If you can show them how to modify their compensation arrangements, resulting in more bottom-line money, you are indeed providing significant value-added. However, to do so requires that you understand the starting point – where they are today and their point of view on compensation.

Sample questions:

- Do you find that often you are not paid for all the time you tend to put into a case?

- How are profits at your firm determined and allocated?

- How do you generally charge your clients?

    ○ Hourly rate, fixed fee, success fee.

- How interested are you in other ways of being paid for your expertise that is not based on the hours you put in?

- How has your compensation changed over the last three years?

- Does your firm market any financial products?

- Do you feel your income is commensurate with your efforts?

- Do you have annual client target profits?

    ○ If yes, what are they?

- Do you receive a bonus?

    ○ What is it based on?

- What are the sources of your revenue?

- Has there been any fluctuation in your income of late?

  ○   What do you attribute it to?

- What is the age of your accounts receivable?

Financial Advisors

Know this. There is not an accountant or attorney who has been in business for a while that has not referred their affluent clients to another financial advisor in the past. You need to understand the whole picture when it comes to the professionals you are considering as strategic partners and their position and experience with financial advisors. This will enable you to best position yourself top-of-mind with an attorney or accountant.

Sample questions:

- How many financial advisors are you currently working with?

- What has been your best and worst experience working with a financial advisor?

  ○   How do you prefer working with a financial advisor?

- Do you have a preference for dealing with independent versus a large company's financial advisor?

- With how many financial advisors have you shared professional relationships?

- Do you serve on a Board of Advisors of any financial advisor?

  ○   Do they refer clients to you?

- What is your criterion for the "ideal advisor?"

- Do you have undivided loyalty to any other financial advisors?

  ○   What is it based on?

- Do you refer business?

  ◦ Is there reciprocity?

- On what topics/subjects do you seek their expertise?

  ◦ What effect have these financial advisors had on your revenue?

- Are you part of a financial advisor's study group?

- How did your clients find their existing financial advisors?

- Who have you worked with in the last 12 months?

The Close

The overarching objective is to create a pipeline of new affluent clients by becoming strategic partners with an accountant or attorney. Therefore, you will need to determine if a particular professional is amenable to the idea of working closely with you.

Sample questions:

- Would you be interested in working together to better serve your clients and make your practice more successful?

- How do you feel about someone like me helping you enhance your practice?

  ◦ What are the best ways for me to be a resource for you?

- What value do you receive from my process?

  ◦ Financially?

  ◦ Time?

  ◦ Simplicity of life?

- How can I help to make you more money?

- What do I need to do to become your strategic partner?

- Could you see yourself working with me?

- What would it take for you to refer business to me?

- Is there a reason you would not refer me to a client?

- What is the next step?

Your Objective Using the Professional Profiling Tool

By conducting the professional profile, you will learn if the particular professional would make a good strategic partner for you. It is the norm in the financial advisory industry to "sell yourself" to accountants and attorneys. Our perspective – across the board – is that you are a marketer, not a sales person. By using the professional profiling tool, you will find the accountants and attorneys as well as other types of professionals who will enable you to build a very successful practice with affluent clients.

To reiterate, you are the one selecting your strategic partners. You are going to help them to be more successful. Therefore, you are doing the choosing. And, all you need to choose is FIVE (see *Chapter 7, Five Strategic Shifts*).

The other essential result of using the professional profiling tool is that you will be able to identify the economic glue that is crucial to creating the pipeline. Experience using the professional profiling tool will enable you to readily spot where you can add value to a professional's practice. The only way you will be able to add value is to know what would be of significant value to a particular professional. And, by employing the professional profiling tool, you will uncover their definitions of "value."

To ensure we're all on the same page, the three-fold purpose of the professional profiling tool is:

- ***Rapport Building.*** Make meaningful personal connections with a potential partner.

- ***Evaluate Potential.*** Are they a viable and valuable partner? Do they have clients of the wealth level you desire? Are they willing and able to refer?

- ***Add Value.*** Hunt for ways to add value, by searching for a potential strategic partner's problems or goals. Problems you can help them solve. Goals you can help them achieve. Do this and you are on your way to becoming their strategic partner.

The Implementation Roadmap

In coaching financial advisors to become rainmakers, we've found a solid number of them are helped by seeing the way the process often initially plays out. Moreover, we've found that many financial advisors want to know just how, in the beginning, to bring the Professional Profiling Tool to bear. The answer is the implementation road map – it's the steps you need to take to get started (Exhibit 9.1).

Exhibit 9.1: The Implementation Roadmap

Step#7: Meet Top Prospects

Step#6: Post Meeting Brief & Next Steps

Step#5: Meet Potential Strategic Partners

Step#4: Practice Profiling

Step#3: Prepare to Profile

Step#2: Rank Prospects

Step#1: Establish List of Potential Partners

What follows is a series of action steps that culminate in providing a financial advisor a linear track to prepare for forging strategic partnerships with professionals. The end goal of this process is to generate affluent client referrals by finding a way to add value to a professional's business.

Step #1: Establish List of Potential Partners. Establish a list of potential strategic partners. Your list of potential partners should be gathered primarily from two sources:

- Attorneys and accountants that have sent referrals over in the past (affiliations).

- Professionals that you are aware of, but have no present referral exchange, but can be accessed. In thinking of these professionals, do not limit yourself to attorneys and accountants.

You should also consider other professionals with whom you have no connection but believe to have strong potential. Do not list more than 10 prospects, as your list becomes unwieldy.

Step #2: Rank Prospects. Numerically rank these prospects by potential, "1" is best, "10" is lowest. Potential should be regarded as the professional's ability to refer quality clients as well as their willingness to refer based on what you know about them so far.

We fully recognize that prior to meeting them you will likely have imperfect knowledge of these facts at this stage. However, we want you to attempt to order them so that you can start this process with low potential strategic partner prospects, ramping up on the process and gaining skill along the way, prior to going after your best strategic partner prospects.

Remember that in an existing affiliation (you have given 10 referrals, they have given you one or none), specific behavior patterns and roles become established in people's minds. This creates a form of "relationship inertia" where the professional may be very resistant to change. You can try to change them, but if you find yourself expending energy without any change, remember the word N.E.X.T.

Step #3: Preparing to Use the Professional Profiling Tool. The professional profiling tool is jam packed with potential questions you might ask. You don't want to ask all the questions or even a random number of them. On the contrary, you want to be prepared with what you believe are your high-impact questions.

Accordingly, to create the best chance of success, review the questions we provided (see above) with a highlighter in hand. Highlight questions that resonate with you. Write down any additional questions that you think might be valuable.

Step #4: Practice Using the Professional Profiling Tool. Once you have your hit list of questions, begin to practice on a branch manager, your general agent, a colleague, a co-worker – anyone who is willing to help you. If possible, make this person your "accountability partner," or if you have a professional coach use him or her.

Don't go robotic on this. It's not a flow chart of "if-thens." One of the Elite 1200 uses the following metaphor: "The conversation should flow like water, following the path of least resistance to a client, a problem, or a goal." Ultimately, this is an open-ended conversation. Remember, you have become highly skilled at a very analogous process over the years with your affluent clients. Now, you want to employ the same skill set, but simply move it over to "centers of influence."

Step #5: Meetings with Potential Strategic Partners. Start meeting with your potential strategic partners. It is recommended that you start with prospect #5 or #6 to gain real world expertise prior to going after your top prospects (#1 or #2). This way, if there are any "glitches," they can be worked out before approaching the "best" prospects.

Step #6: Post Meeting Brief and Next Step Planning. Review the meeting outcome of prospects #5 or #6 with your accountability partner. Describe your actions, their responses, the outcomes, and next steps. Send a brief hand written note to the professional you met with, nothing fancy or elaborate, just a polite acknowledgement. Remember they are your clients.

Step #7: Meetings with Top Prospects. Meet with your top prospect
potential strategic partners. Having gained real world expertise with
prospects #5 and #6, now you will be better prepared to target your
top prospects (#1 or #2).

Conclusions

Your detailed knowledge of strategic partners is critical to your success as a rainmaker. It's essential to your ability to join the ranks of the
Elite 1200. Without question, the most effective systematic methodology
to gaining that detailed knowledge is the professional profiling tool.

By collecting information in the nine categories of the professional
profiling tool, you'll be able to paint a complete picture of the professional. Initially, the information will tell you if this professional is worth
your time and effort, or should you just say N.E.X.T. By being able to
quickly screen prospective strategic partners, you'll be saving yourself a
great deal of time and effort.

Using the professional profiling tool, you'll subsequently be able to
determine where you can add value through indirect financial incentives.
It's indirect financial incentives (see *Chapter 10, The Economic Glue*)
that will enable you to effectively work with five strategic partners. What
these incentives need to be for a particular professional is relatively easy
to uncover using this approach. So, now let's turn to what holds strategic
partnerships together.

Chapter 10

The Economic Glue

"Treat a person as he is, and he will remain as he is. Treat him as he could be, and he will become what he should be."
— Jimmy Johnson

By this point, you have convinced your strategic partners of your qualifications on the basics – personal integrity and technical expertise. You have also profiled them so you know if they're the "right" professionals for you to be concentrating on. Your profiling has also helped you build rapport as well as direct you to the appropriate economic glue for that professional.

Now it is time to apply the economic glue to bind the partnership together. Notice that the basics do come first. Don't rush in with suggestions of economic incentives before you really understand the professional and have attended to the basics.

Now that we are moving beyond the basics, it's the time for value-added. Now is when you should think about the sorts of "economic glue" you can apply to create stronger bonds between your strategic partners and yourself. As we'll reiterate, when you become more adept in using the professional profiling tool, you will find it easier and easier to discern the appropriate economic glue for each accountant, attorney, or other professional you choose to partner with.

All in all, the emphasis on financial incentives is appropriate, because that is what these professionals need most. You will recall earlier data where we discussed the outlook for accountants and attorneys. When asked what their concerns were, the top concern was downward pressure on their personal incomes. For the most part, these professionals feel they need to make more money. That is why we focus on financial incentives within the strategic partnership.

There are two types of financial incentives. Direct financial incentives generate revenues for the professional immediately, and they are attractive to professionals. However, direct financial incentives are usually impossible for financial advisors to consistently provide to their strategic partners. By contrast, indirect financial incentives are not limited in the same way, and they are as valuable to accountants, attorneys, and other professionals. We will take you through the entire incentives package step by step, including:

- *Direct Financial Incentives*

  ○ Reciprocal referrals.

  ○ Sharing in the revenues from product sales.

  ○ Generating significant professional fees.

- *Indirect Financial Incentives*

  ○ Practice management.

  ○ Insights into alternative compensation structures.

  ○ Marketing support and ideas.

Direct Financial Incentives

There are a number of ways financial advisors can provide direct financial incentives to accountants and attorneys. These include incentives that result in new income for the strategic partner. The three most pervasive are:

- Reciprocal referrals.

- Sharing in the revenues from product sales.

- Generating significant professional fees.

Reciprocal referrals. The vast majority of attorneys and accountants make their money by billing out their time. They are struggling to grow their practices. As a result, many are looking for reciprocal referrals from the financial advisor. In our studies, most attorneys (54.0%) and accountants (62.2%) agreed that reciprocal referrals were "very" or "extremely" important (Exhibit 10.1).

Exhibit 10.1: Importance of Reciprocal Client Referrals

N = 619 private client attorneys; 251 accountants

Source: Creating a Pipeline of New Affluent Clients (2003).

While reciprocal client referrals are a powerful "economic glue" and one the financial advisor can provide, attorneys (4.7%) and accountants (7.6%) tend to strongly recognize that one-for-one wealthy client referrals are not a realistic expectation (Exhibit 10.2). The reason is that attorneys and accountants recognize that most financial advisors do not have as many appropriate clients or the same level of power in the relationship as they do. This is the very same reason they tend to refer to multiple financial advisors when they have not been exposed to any other form of economic glue besides trading referrals.

Exhibit 10.2: Do Not Believe Financial Advisors Can Trade Referrals One-for-One

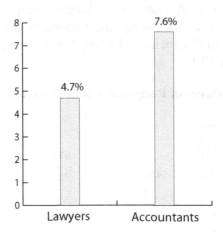

N = 619 private client attorneys; 251 accountants

Source: Creating a Pipeline of New Affluent Clients (2003).

Sharing in the revenues from product sales. At the current time, relatively few attorneys (9.2%) are seeking direct revenue participation (Exhibit 10.3). While this is a small proportion, revenue sharing is a new phenomenon for attorneys and a very significant one. Some attorneys are part of multi-disciplinary practices in order to participate in revenues from product sales. However, recent research shows that attorneys, on the whole, are actually moving away from sharing in the revenues generated from the sale of financial products. The best estimate is that, today, no more than 5% of private client lawyers are sharing in the revenues from product sales.

As for accountants, none of them (0.0%) are interested in sharing in the product sale revenues. However, remember, here we are only considering those accountants who are not themselves financial advisors. Some accountants have already made the move to be financial advisors, and so they share in the revenues from the sale of financial products. Overall, no more than 20% of accountants are licensed and this percentage is likely to be stable for some time to come.

Exhibit 10.3: Share of Financial Advisor Revenues from Product Sales

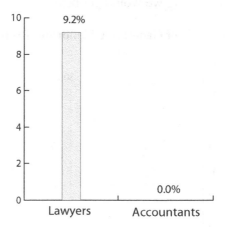

N = 619 private client attorneys; 251 accountants

Source: Creating a Pipeline of New Affluent Clients (2003).

Although there is a growing number of attorneys establishing multi-disciplinary practices and accountants who share in the revenue from product sales, we project that most professionals will not share in the revenues. As we look forward over the next three years, all indications are that most accountants and attorneys will **not** be getting licensed to accept fees or commissions on product sales. Accordingly, it follows that you will need to rely predominantly on some other form of economic glue.

Generating professional fees. Another way for financial advisors to be reciprocated for affluent client referrals from attorneys and accountants is to find a way to generate new professional fees (Exhibit 10.4). A financial advisor may hire the attorney to perform legal work (such as research or document review) or hire the accountant for tax related services. More attorneys (25.0%) and accountants (30.7%) favor this approach than like the idea of direct revenue sharing, perhaps because it sets up a boundary around the legal or accounting work provided.

We have come across some financial advisors that hire the professional themselves for this same purpose. Perhaps the most extreme of these examples was one financial advisor who said he was getting his taxes prepared seven times by seven different accountants. He wasn't

looking for the best tax return. This must have been a system that worked
for him, but not something we would get behind.

Exhibit 10.4: Importance of Generating Significant Professional Fees

N = 619 private client attorneys; 251 accountants

Source: Creating a Pipeline of New Affluent Clients (2003).

This approach has been criticized. Some raise a question whether
a financial advisor is generating a need for bona fide legal advice or
accounting services or just creating busy work. Put another way, is generating significant legal fees or accounting services just a backdoor method
to share a financial advisor's revenues? Compensation through the generation of legal fees or accounting services is as much of an ethical issue
for an attorney or accountant as direct revenue participation. You can
sidestep these issues before they become problems by working through
issues of professional integrity with your strategic partners.

Indirect Financial Incentives

Indirect financial incentives are another, high potential, form of economic glue. Indirect financial incentives are ways financial advisors can
add value through practice support to the professional, value that in many
instances outstrips the value that even fee sharing can create. Indirect
financial incentives include the information, insights, and experience that

financial advisors can provide to an attorney's or accountant's practice. Indirect financial incentives have the advantage of being relatively free of the ethical issues that can constrain some professionals.

Indirect financial incentives can be interesting. Lawyers and accountants can easily and effectively discriminate among financial advisors on this basis. Some financial advisors are very good in this area and can provide meaningful value-added to their strategic partners. Other financial advisors are not as strong and are less attractive to professionals. When indirect incentives work well, they result in a stronger bond between the financial advisor and the attorney or accountant. Even more importantly, they enable everyone to better serve the affluent client. Indirect financial incentives are the ultimate in value-added knowledge transfer.

Indirect financial incentives have also proven to be the best way to create relationships with other professionals who are not private client attorneys or accountants. The ability to use direct financial incentives with these other professionals is exceedingly limited. And, to split revenues on products requires licensing and disclosure that is anathema to the vast majority of these professionals.

It's important to note that we are not against fee sharing. If you go this route and it's working, that's great. However, the research reveals that most professionals do not engage in this process. Hence, to exclusively focus on this route is like buying a lottery ticket. It looks attractive, but can often be a mirage. Additionally, we are not against trading clients or generating professional fees. However, these are indicative of affiliations, which are less productive than strategic partnerships.

The three critical areas where you can provide indirect financial incentives for the accountants and attorneys you have as strategic partners are:

- Practice management.

- Insights into alternative compensation structures.

- Marketing support and ideas.

Practice Management

When it comes to practice management considerations, most attorneys (86.1%) and accountants (89.2%) are looking for best practice insights (Exhibit 10.5). Making a practice more effective is considered a very valuable form of value-added. There is widespread recognition among professionals of how beneficial more information on best practices would be. Professionals recognize that they could better take advantage of the opportunities that exist with wealthy clients if they simply had more support.

Exhibit 10.5: Interest in "Best Practices"

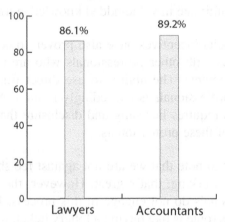

N = 619 private client attorneys; 251 accountants

Source: Creating a Pipeline of New Affluent Clients (2003).

Because you have already developed an in-depth understanding of their business models (see *Chapter 9, The Professional Profiling Tool*), you are in a position to share with them ways they can improve their practices. The way to proceed is to link up resources you know about to their needs.

Consider the concept of "professional style." Professional style is a framework for analyzing the business models of private client attorneys. We can readily see opportunities for financial advisors who are able to show attorneys the economic returns of the four different professional styles. The follow-up is to support them as they transition their practices to a more profitable professional style.

Let's describe the professional styles concept in more detail so you can see how indirect value added can work. The professional styles framework classified attorneys on the basis of how they respond to their wealthy clients:

- The Technician.

- The Rainmaker.

- The Experimenter.

- The Entrepreneur.

These professional styles encompass the types of legal services these attorneys provide, the way they provide them, and the way their practices operate. Most importantly, these professional styles have a direct bearing on how financially successful the attorneys are. The average compensation for some styles is significantly greater than it is for others. Among attorneys, nearly two-thirds are *Technicians,* one in five are *Rainmakers,* and one in ten are *Experimenters. Entrepreneurs,* fewer than one in ten, are the smallest group (Exhibit 10.6).

Exhibit 10.6: Types of Layers

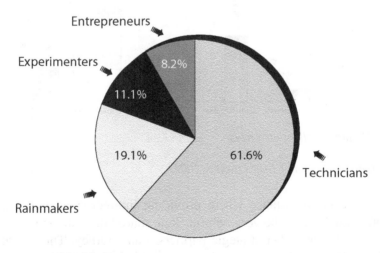

N = 619 private client attorneys

Source: The Private Client Lawyer (2003).

Over the past three years, the average annual income of the 619 private client attorneys we surveyed was $284,000. Note that the median income was $192,000; this indicates wide variation among private client attorneys in terms of earnings. That is, some especially highly compensated attorneys pull the average up (Exhibit 10.7).

Entrepreneurs were far and away the biggest earners (mean income = $1,274,000; median income = $782,000). *Rainmakers* were next on the income ladder (mean income = $538,000; median income = $404,000). Their approach was to originate business and generate leverage through other attorneys. *Experimenters* followed with a mean income of $151,000 and median income of $109,000. Finally, the *Technicians* were the lowest earners (mean income = $97,000; median income = $62,000) and their income was based almost exclusively on billable hours.

Exhibit 10.7: Pre-Tax Income

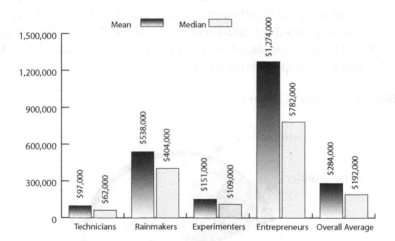

N = 619 private client attorneys

Source: The Private Client Lawyer (2003).

Here is an instance where providing indirect financial support to professionals could be very helpful. Jane shared the data on professional styles with one of her strategic partners – an attorney. This led to them going into great detail about his practice, his lack of ability to grow his income, and his absolute need to make changes. The attorney turned out to be an exceptionally adept Technician. He understood the need to move to becoming a Rainmaker.

Jane and the attorney initially engaged in a number of *strategic scenario sessions* where the attorney's clients were assessed (see *Chapter 11, Filling the Pipeline*). The result of these sessions was significantly more legal business for the attorney from his existing clients. These sessions also resulted in nine new clients for Jane to the tune of about $62 million in new assets to be managed, as well as five life insurance policies with an aggregate face value of $126 million. All of this started with a discussion of the professional styles of private client attorneys.

Let's look at another example, this one focused on accountants. Although we have been talking about traditional accountants, there are opportunities for creating strategic partnerships among accountants who have already added financial services to their practices. There are a number of ways you can help such firms be more successful and, consequently, do more business with you. In this example, the answers lie in what it takes these accountants to build successful financial services practices (Exhibit 10.8).

Exhibit 10.8: What it Takes for Accountants to Build Successful Financial Services Practices

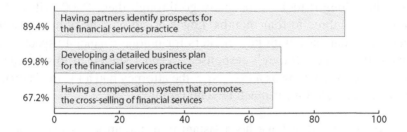

N = 824 accountants providing financial products

Source: Accountants as Wealth Managers (2002).

If you share information like this with accountants who are trying to build financial services practices, you are helping them better understand the tools and perspectives they will need to master. The logic is that by helping them develop successful business models, you can help make them more successful. They will reciprocate, which will make your practice more successful.

Kevin did indeed share this information with a boutique accounting firm specializing in franchise owners. He applied the very same planning approach he used in establishing and growing his own financial advisory firm with the accounting firm. The result was that they ended up creating another firm – a joint-venture between his own firm and the accounting firm. Then using *strategic scenario sessions*, Kevin was able to identify the clients of the accountants that were most worthwhile for him to see. And, the accountants then set up the meetings.

Let us close with a very simple, but powerful example, utilizing a tool that virtually every financial advisor in the country uses, as the economic glue. Lewis sought ways to add value to a trusts and estates attorney's practice. He profiled him on how he created his billable hours.

The attorney did two things. First, he contacted his clients every five years to remind them to come in for an update to their estate plan. Secondly, when there was a significant change to a tax law, he would review his client base (2000+ Estate Plans) for clients that this law would affect, and then the attorney would send out letters to these clients to tell them they should come in to update their estate plan. He was in the process of notifying his clients about a tax law change to large IRA's. Lewis asked how long it took to manually go through these 2000+ files? The attorney said three to four months. Lewis asked why he didn't have the clients in a database with key markers for unique financial aspects, like a large IRA. The attorney's response, "When I started in this business, there was no such thing as a PC." Now the attorney had a PC in his office, he just hadn't used it for much beyond typing.

Lewis offered to have his assistant train the attorney's assistant on utilizing a database to track and analyze the attorney's client base when tax law changes occurred. Now, what took the attorney three to four months, takes three to four seconds. A massive amount of time and effort has been saved, and the attorney's letters to clients go out in a much more timely fashion.

By looking at these three examples, we have shown how to address the practice management aspect to add value to the accountants and attorneys you are seeking to bring into strategic partnerships. These professionals are on the constant lookout for practice management tools and ideas, and you can bring insights to them.

They are also seeking processes that they can employ with their wealthy clients. This is another area where you can provide economic glue. Nine out of ten accountants (90.4%) who are not providing financial products are very interested in learning about highly effective systematic processes for use with wealthy clients (Exhibit 10.9). This, of course, begins with a demonstrable understanding of the wealthy (see *Chapter 2, The Affluent*). However, it goes beyond just knowing about the wealthy. It moves to having a process that the professional sees as systematic and reliable.

Exhibit 10.9: Accountants Are Very Interested in Learning about Processes

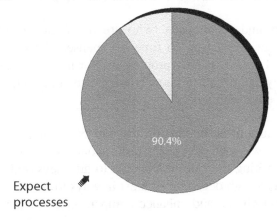

Expect processes

N = 251 accountants

Source: Creating a Pipeline of New Affluent Clients (2003).

In looking over a process that you provide them, accountants and attorneys will bear two criteria in mind. They will want any such piece of value-added you propose to meet both criteria. These criteria are:

- That the process is "intuitively correct."

- That it is logical and methodical.

By "intuitively correct" we mean that it has to make sense to the professional. It has to fit with the professional's sense of how services are provided and how clients react. It cannot be a radical departure from what the professional is already doing, and it should sound "right" when you explain it. The immediate reaction of the professional has to be: "Yes, this would work."

For a process to meet the second criteria, it has to be logical and methodical. It has to be simple enough to draw as you talk it out with the attorney or accountant. A process is graphically depicted as a flow chart or a pictogram of some kind so, of course, you can draw it. If you can't draw it, you probably do not have a process. It would be wise to practice drawing and explaining the processes you are considering proposing to a strategic partner.

Insights Into Alternative Compensation Structures

Most attorneys and accountants (who are not financial advisors) predominantly charge fees based on time + expenses. This traditional compensation model is increasingly problematic for these professionals; it restricts what they can do. Professionals are not the only ones limited by traditional compensation models.

There is more and more interest on the part of affluent clients for different, alternative ways of paying for professional services. Affluent clients have been making their desires known to attorneys and accountants. Today there is a high degree of interest in ways to improve billing practices for affluent clients and enhance compensation for the professional (Exhibit 10.10).

Exhibit 10.10: Interest in Ways to Improve Compensation Structures

N = 619 private client attorneys; 251 accountants

Source: Creating a Pipeline of New Affluent Clients (2003).

One of the compensation options that is capturing a great deal of interest from professionals is value-based fees. Value-based fees allow attorneys and accountants more latitude to bill based on the value that the client has received, instead of on a fixed hourly rate. We have seen financial advisors be very effective in helping accountants and attorneys understand and apply value-based fee structures in selected instances. The benefits of value-based fees are many, and include:

- *A matter of expertise.* Value-based fees provide appropriate compensation to the professional for delivering requisite expertise.

- *Affluent-client centered.* Because of how they are structured, value-based fees enable attorneys and accountants to be focused on their wealthy clients, not on billing.

- *Affluent clients equate certain costs with value.* In order to charge value-based fees, a professional must justify them through communication with the affluent client.

- *Prompts action.* By charging value-based fees, the affluent client is positively disposed to implement the attorney's or accountant's recommendations.

Value-based fees are project fees where the benefits to the affluent client are clearly communicated in advance. This communication includes a checklist of defined activities that the attorney or accountant will undertake as well as an enumeration of the deliverables provided to the wealthy client. Professionals who are convinced of the value they provide and who are able to communicate that value potential to their affluent clients are in an excellent position to profit from value-based fees. Importantly, their wealthy clients benefit as well.

The value-based approach represents a cultural change from the traditional time + expense compensation model. And while the case for making the transition to value-based fees is compelling, many professionals – even those who dislike the time + expenses model – are understandably cautious. For wealthy clients and professionals alike, there are four misconceptions that are keeping them from seeing the benefits of value-based fees. They are:

- *Failing to understand the perceived value that is the basis of the fee.* We have found that many attorneys and accountants do not truly appreciate the considerable value they deliver.

- *Failing to understand the cost structure of delivering high-quality advice.* In order to quote a price from the beginning and make money requires a precise understanding of the professional firm's cost structure and a clear idea of the talent and resource requirements.

- *Failing to translate the benefits of their advice into value for the affluent client.* Affluent clients need to understand the value they receive for the fees they are charged. This process is a marketing function and must be recognized as such.

- *Fear of the affluent client saying "no."* In value-based fee structures, the project cost given to the wealthy client tends to be much higher than the traditional estimate. As a result, many professionals fear that the wealthy client will balk at the cost and decide not to proceed.

Although relatively new to the legal and accounting professions, value-based fees are frequently used in other advisory businesses. As a result, the process for constructing value-based fee structures is well developed. In fact, there are a variety of different methodologies that can be applied, and you will want to be knowledgeable about the major types.

We have developed a case study to show you the impact of, and client reaction to, value-based fees. We worked with one of our clients (an accounting firm in this instance) to conduct a systematic study of value-based fees in operation (Exhibit 10.11). We created a methodology to compare and contrast traditional time-based pricing versus value-based pricing in a formal field experiment. We selected 20 representative wealthy clients and created proposals for doing advanced planning for each. The pricing for each of the 20 cases was worked up using both approaches. As computed, the value-based fees worked out to be an average of 39.2% higher than the time-based fees.

The 20 cases were then randomly divided into two groups of ten clients each. In one group, each wealthy client was given the proposal with the estimated time-based fee structure. In the other group, each client was offered the value-based fee. The affluent clients who were presented with the value-based fee proposal were told what deliverables they would receive and the rationale for the fees based on the value that the client would receive. The affluent clients who received the time-based proposals were told the rationale for the cost in terms of the amount of time the accountant believed the planning would take and explained what the wealthy prospect should expect in terms of that time.

Four out of ten of the wealthy prospects that were offered the time-based approach decided to go forward with the planning. In contrast, nine out of ten clients who were presented with the value-based approach authorized that the work be done. For the affluent clients accepting the value-based fee model, the accounting firm generated $338,000 more in revenue than they would have using the time-based approach.

Exhibit 10.11: Results of Field Experiment in Value-Based versus Traditional Pricing for Professional Services

Factor	Traditional Fee Group	Value-Based Fee Group
Number of affluent clients approached with advanced planning proposals	10	10
Estimated fee	X	X plus 39.2%
Number of affluent clients who decided to go ahead	4	9
Revenue to the accounting firm as a result of the process	X	X plus $338,000

The field experiment shows us several things. First, affluent clients do not object to paying for expertise, provided that they realize that there is real value being delivered. If they stand to gain by X, they understand that it makes sense to invest some percentage of X in the advisor. Second, value-based advisory fees actually engender wealthy client compliance with advisory recommendations; affluent clients who pay more for advice value it more and tend to comply more readily with recommendations. The third benefit is that the process of creating value-based pricing forces the professional to become much more focused on the benefits accruing to the affluent client. Finally, when real value is being delivered, it enhances the quality of the relationship between the professional and the wealthy client. Properly structured advisory fees actually help build a stronger relationship with the wealthy, as well as generate significant revenue and referrals. The critical proviso is that real value must be added and effectively communicated.

Adopting a Project Fee Compensation Model

We showed how transitioning from a time + expenses compensation model to a project compensation model makes accountants more money – when they do it correctly. A financial advisor used this insight to create – what a number of accounting firms and law firms considered – tremendous value for them.

With the assistance of an investment banking associate at his firm, the financial advisor sat down with the partner-in-charge of the trusts and estates department of a mid-sized law firm. Using the time sheets of the partners and associates they were able to derive the average fees for a number of more common estate planning deliverables (e.g., estate plans, wills, various trusts, even entire somewhat complex estate plans).

The law firm then took these prices and added about 15% more. Then over the following eight months, the law firm used them instead of the time + expenses compensation model. What they found was that the trusts and estates department was nearly 25% more profitable on a per client basis. While the trusts and estates department fully adopted the new compensation model for "routine" deliverables, they maintained their time + expenses compensation model for the more affluent clients with especially complex financial and personal situations.

For the financial advisor, the benefit of adding this kind of value was astounding. First, he did not get any business from anyone at the law firm for a little more than half a year. It took that long for the attorneys to see and understand the financial benefits of the project fee compensation model. So, from when he was first given the time sheets till the time he started to see his payoff, more than a year and a half went by. However, after the attorneys realized the value of what he brought to the table, the gates swung wide open.

Over the subsequent year, he received over 21 affluent client referrals. Out of those 21 referrals, 16 of them (76.2%) became investment management clients. On average, each of these affluent clients provides $3.3 million to manage for a total of $56.1 million. At the same time, for 12 of the 21, he wrote their life insurance for a total of $622,000 in first year commissions. And, year two started off at a faster pace.

Because of the success of his value-added approach with the trusts and estates department, he and the investment banker are seeing what they can do with the real estate and corporate finance departments. To date, he hasn't seen any referrals from these departments. However, his experience with the trusts and estates department confirms the need to be patient.

Marketing Support and Ideas

Another way in which financial advisors can deliver value-added to attorneys and accountants is by providing marketing ideas and support. This is a way for attorneys and accountants to get more wealthy clients without depending on referrals from financial advisors. That explains why, in our research, about two-thirds of the attorneys (64.3%) and three-quarters of the accountants (73.3%) were "very" or "extremely" interested in marketing ideas and support (Exhibit 10.12).

Exhibit 10.12: Importance of Marketing Ideas and Support

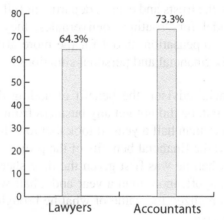

N = 619 private client attorneys; 251 accountants

Source: Creating a Pipeline of New Affluent Clients (2003).

Marketing ideas and support come in a wide variety of forms. To be valuable to strategic partners, marketing support has to result in increased wealthy client business as well as better relationships with affluent clients. Strategic partners have little use for marketing ideas that do not yield benefits in the form of clients.

Marketing ideas and support can take many forms. They could include improving yield per client, or they could result in an increase of wealthy clients. They could focus on profitability or revenue per client or on building a better product platform.

We can illustrate another approach to providing marketing support. A number of the Elite 1200 share with their strategic partners the way they work with their affluent clients. One of the Elite 1200 has taught his strategic partners how to use high-net-worth psychology (see *Chapter 2, The Affluent*). However, the attorneys and accountants he works with are still uneasy when it comes to identifying which of the nine high-net-worth personalities a wealthy person is. They regularly ask the financial advisor with help on this matter, which brings him into a discussion of the affluent client immediately. Many times this translates into business for him.

More Examples of Indirect Financial Incentives

In coaching financial advisors, one-on-one and in workshops, on becoming rainmakers, we've seen a wide variety of ways they have been able to add-value. The results have been a steady stream of new affluent clients for them as well as more business for their strategic partners. In this section, we'll provide a number of additional examples describing the indirect financial incentives these financial advisors employed.

Example #1:

Mary was trying to build a partnership with a trusts and estates attorney. She ran the professional profile and discovered this attorney was concerned about his income. She asked the attorney what kind of marketing he did. The attorney said none. He operated on billable hours, and his clients think he's trying to run the meter if he calls.

Mary asked how many clients he had. The attorney answered that he had about 2,000, bearing in mind that a more apt description of these clients would be files with older estate plans. A good rule of thumb on the expiration date for an estate plan is somewhere between 3 and 7 years. Mary quickly realized that the odds of a large number of those 2,000 plans being wildly past their expiration date were pretty good. The challenge became how she could help this attorney convert the latent billable hours of these out of date estate plans into income for the attorney – and business for her.

She came up with a simple but brilliant drip marketing strategy to help the clients realize how old their estate plan was. She hired a graphic designer for a couple hundred dollars to develop 15 birthday cards, not for a human being but rather to mark the age of the estate plan itself. This way the clients would be annually reminded of how old their plan was getting and the need for updating it. This in turn would increase billable hours, and in return the attorney made Mary the exclusive financial advisor he would refer his clients to.

Example #2

Neville, a financial advisor in the DC area received two extremely good referrals from a divorce attorney. Then the referrals dried up. Almost a year went by without any referrals, so he called up the attorney and invited him to lunch. Through the course of lunch, Neville asked the attorney why he hadn't given him any referrals lately. The attorney became irritated. He responded, "I have helped your business a great deal, you've done nothing for me, why should I give you any?"

Neville began to profile the attorney to learn how he could help him. He discovered the attorney was sending out his P&L statements to be run, incurring a cost for this service. He had the ability to do this for the attorney, and took that cost off his practice. In return, the attorney began to make referrals, when appropriate, to Neville.

Example #3

A financial advisor on the west coast was using a highly effective seminar on how to become more financially savvy with the female prospects in the general public. The seminar was very successful at converting attendees to one-on-one appointments. However, there was a problem. This advisor had just raised her account minimum, wanting to move up market focusing on wealthier clients.

The seminar was bringing her many clients, but not at the wealth level she wanted. So she began to meet with accountants to find out how she could get referrals. She met one accountant that was very eager to get more clients, and was already serving the wealth level of clients she was seeking.

Then it hit this financial advisor. She could run this seminar on behalf of the accountant. Anybody would be a good client for the accountant for tax preparation, let alone other tax related services he could provide. The financial advisor ran the seminar for the accountant three times, and got him over 40 new clients. In return she got an agreement from the accountant to make her the sole referring financial advisor when appropriate for his wealthier clients.

Example #4

One financial advisor built a partnership with a divorce attorney in the following way. Differentiation from other top divorce attorneys is a major issue. This financial advisor profiled the divorce attorney discovering that his clients were wealthy, female, and usually with children. The profiling process enabled the financial advisor to identify a key concern of the divorce attorney's clients as a point of differentiation.

When a wealthy couple divorces, the assets that they want to set aside and preserve for their children typically go into a trust. This potentially creates a moral hazard for the child by giving them knowledge that they will one day, quite young, become instantly wealthy. This is very commonly a grave concern of both parents. Realizing this, the financial advisor brought in an expert on raising financially fit children that is adept at working with heirs of the wealthy to help them develop a healthy money outlook. When meeting with clients, the three present themselves as a team that will respectively allay the top three concerns of the divorcing spouse – the divorce, their assets, and their kid's "money health." This has helped the divorce attorney win more wealthy clients and the financial advisor to become the strategic partner of the attorney.

Example #5

O'Neil built a partnership with a trusts and estates attorney working with high-end clients by pioneering this idea to differentiate the trusts and estates attorney's practice from his competitors while in the prospecting stage. O'Neil identified an archivist, a personal historian that interviews a wealthy person to learn their life history, their experiences, their values, and the wisdom they'd like to impart to their heirs, and then distills this information into a small book that is given to the wealthy clients and their heirs at the reading of their will. He recognized that he could bring this service into the equation as the trusts and estates attorney pitched his services to wealthy prospects, helping the attorney to best his competition.

To be clear, this service may be nothing more than a giant ego trip for the very wealthy. Regardless, it helped the trusts and estates attorney to get the business. And, O'Neil significantly benefited by the affluent clients the attorney referred who needed life insurance.

Conclusions

For relationships to prosper over the long term, they have to be win-win. If you want to win by creating a pipeline of new affluent clients from an accountant or attorney or some other type of professional, you need to know what you will give them that they will think is a win.

In this chapter, we propose that you cement the relationship by applying economic glue. We break this economic glue down into direct financial incentives (these include reciprocal referrals, sharing in the revenues from product sales, and generating significant professional fees) and indirect financial incentives (including practice management, insights into alternative compensation structures, and marketing support and ideas).

To a large degree, your ability to enhance the business building initiatives of accountants and attorneys is the most effective way for you to add value to their practices. The extent to which you can enable them to better serve their high-net-worth clients, or obtain more new affluent clients for them, will place you in very good stead.

What you've done so far is construct a pipeline for new affluent clients to be directed to you. What you now need to do is ensure that this pipeline is full and remains that way.

Chapter 11

Filling the Pipeline

"When a team outgrows individual performance and learns team confidence, excellency becomes a reality."

– Joe Paterno

You have a strategic partner who is an accountant or an attorney or another type of professional who doesn't do what you do well and is willing to partner with you. Furthermore, you've started to receive new affluent client referrals from your strategic partner. Every time an opportunity presents itself, your strategic partner directs a wealthy client your way. You recognize this is a joint-venture referral, but you know that in all likelihood the affluent client will do business with you.

In return, you are providing some combination of indirect financial incentives to your strategic partner. Usually you're helping your strategic partner with marketing and/or practice management. Your efforts are beginning to make a meaningful difference in the success of the practice of your strategic partner. Of course, when the opportunity arises, you'll send one of your wealthy clients in need of the expertise of your strategic partner to him or her. However, your focus is on indirect financial incentives.

So far, so good. However, this isn't enough. At this point you're out of the gate strong, but it's a long race. While being top of mind – while your strategic partner is always considering if an affluent client he or she is seeing would be a good fit for you – what you need is for your strategic partner to dig into his or her affluent client base and find the appropriate high-net-worth client to refer to you. Then, your strategic partner has to arrange for you – under optimal conditions – to meet those wealthy clients.

You need your strategic partner to be extremely proactive, not just reactive (which is the norm). When you have convinced and motivated your strategic partner to go searching for affluent clients who will benefit from your services, you have your consistent stream of new wealthy clients. We call this: *filling the pipeline.*

In order to join the ranks of the Elite 1200, you'll need to see many wealthy clients who are interested in what you have to offer and want to do business now. Experience shows us it's critical to see many affluent clients, because there's no guarantee that every one referred to you by your strategic partner will click with you and avail themselves of what you can provide. Put another way, it's extremely unlikely that all the wealthy clients your strategic partner refers to you will become your wealthy clients – even though the odds are surely stacked in your favor. At a very basic level, it's still a "numbers game" and that means you have to see a fair number of wealthy potential clients to be able to consistently generate an annual income of $1 million or more.

There are a number of ways to fill the pipeline. In this chapter we'll look at two, the "relatively easier and more direct" approach – *strategic scenario sessions.* The other approach that has proven exceptionally effective is *non-aligned structured seminars.*

Both of these approaches have been field-proven and were developed by members of the Elite 1200 (although we refined them slightly). First, let's consider *strategic scenario sessions.*

Strategic Scenario Sessions

Simply put, *strategic scenario sessions* are those times when you "brainstorm" with your strategic partner about his or her affluent clients. You're not talking about concepts. You're focused directly on clients – wealthy clients. And, in general, the wealthier the clients you're focusing on in *strategic scenario sessions,* the better.

In these *strategic scenario sessions*, you and your strategic partner construct a detailed profile of his or her wealthy clients. As we noted in *Chapter 1, The* Secret *to Sourcing New Affluent Clients*, a defining characteristic of the Elite 1200 is their ability to develop deep understandings of their best clients. What we want to do here is apply that capability to unearth business opportunities with the affluent clients of your strategic partners.

Your ability to discuss products and services in real time – another attribute of the Elite 1200 – is what makes a *strategic scenario session* especially effective. As the two of you are profiling one of his or her affluent clients, you're looking to:

- Identify opportunities for your strategic partner to generate more business.

- Identify opportunities for you to provide financial services and/ or products.

In the process of profiling the wealthy clients of your strategic partner, you need to emphasize the business he or she will garner. Not the business you'll get, but the business your strategic partner will get. This is a critical point. You'll see where you will help the affluent client and consequently make money. You must be very coherent about how your strategic partner will make money. At the same time, it's crucial to always be cognizant and explicit about the value the affluent client will be receiving.

We've found that *strategic scenario sessions*, in themselves, are a form of indirect financial incentives. When done well, these brainstorming sessions prove very profitable for both you and your strategic partner and – more importantly – they result in superior results for the affluent clients profiled. The critical element is to do them properly.

The key to *strategic scenario sessions* is the profiling process. There are many ways to profile affluent clients. Based on our work empirically analyzing the best practices of the Elite 1200, as well as numerous research studies of the behavioral patterns and attitudinal issues of the affluent coupled with coaching financial advisors to reach Elite 1200 status, we've derived an extremely efficacious profiling process – the Whole Client Model.

The Whole Client Model

As its name implies, the Whole Client Model is about the whole person. Even more precisely, for the greater majority of financial advisors, it's about the Whole of the opportunity with each client, getting all, or as much as possible of the wealth management opportunity each client needs.

Whereas most fact-finding systems are skewed to a focus on the assets and related financial information, the Whole Client Model is holistic in nature. Its use will invariably drive you and your strategic partners to uncover opportunity after opportunity for both your offerings and the expertise of your strategic partners.

The Whole Client Model is not only very powerful in the context of *strategic scenario sessions,* it's also at the core of wealth management. Investment oriented financial advisors who transition to a wealth management orientation, which includes adopting the Whole Client Model, see their incomes increase by 35% within the first year. The income increase is, at worst, maintained, but most likely grows – though at a smaller pace.

The Whole Client Model is composed of seven categories. Notice that only one of the seven categories is "Financials" with a few of the other categories rarely if ever included in typical fact-finders.

The following is the seven-sector framework, along with sample questions:

Client

- What is the affluent client's age?

- What is the affluent client's total net worth?

- What is the affluent client's gender?

- What is the affluent client's income?

- What is the affluent client's high-net-worth personality?

Goals & Concerns

- What are the affluent client's quality of life desires? (e.g., houses, travel, boats, cars?)

- What does the affluent client consider his or her top accomplishments to be? What would he or she like them to be?

- What are affluent client's personal goals? What is of central importance to the affluent client personally?

- What does the affluent client worry about?

- What are the affluent client's professional goals? (Short-term and long-term)

- What does the affluent client do for his or her children? What does the affluent client want to do?

- What does the affluent client do for his or her parents? What does the affluent client want to do?

- What does the affluent client do or want to do for other family members or close friends?

- What keeps the affluent client up at night?

- What does the affluent client want to do for society, for the world at large?

- Ideally, where would the affluent client like to be when he or she is 45? 55? 65? 75?

- What are the affluent client's top three concerns?

- What are the affluent client's investment goals? In dollar figures, how much money does he or she need or want?

- If the affluent client did not have to work anymore, what would he or she do?

Relationships

- What family member relationships (spouse, children, brothers/sisters, parents, etc.) are the most important ones in the affluent client's personal and professional life?

- What is the affluent client's religious orientation? How devout is he or she?

- What pets does the affluent client have? How important are these pets?

- How important are the relationships with the people the affluent client works with?

- How important to the affluent client are relationships with people in the community?

- Would the affluent client describe him or herself as an introvert or extrovert?

- What famous people does the affluent client know? How did he or she meet them?

- What schools did the affluent client go to? How important is his or her relationship with these schools?

Financials

- What does the affluent client's investment portfolio look like today?

- How are the non-investable assets structured?

- How does the affluent client make money today? How is that likely to change in the next three years?

- How does the affluent client save or set aside money to invest? How is this likely to change in the next three years?

- What benefits does the affluent client receive from his or her workplace?

- What life insurance does the affluent client have?

- What debts does the affluent client have?

- What property does the affluent client have (e.g., real property, art, jewelry, etc)?

- What new assets does the affluent client expect to receive (e.g. inheritances, stock options) and when?

- What is the affluent client's opinion on taxes? What kinds of taxes bother the client the most?

- When the affluent client thinks about his or her investment portfolio, what are his or her three biggest worries?

- What were the affluent client's best and worst investments? What happened?

Advisors

- Who are the other advisors the affluent client is using? What role does each advisor play?

- Of late, how frequently has the affluent client switched selected advisors?

- What was the affluent client's best and worst experience with an advisor?

- Does the affluent client have a trusts and estates attorney? How does he or she feel about the relationship?

- Does the affluent client have a life insurance agent? How does he or she feel about the relationship?

- Does the affluent client have an accountant? How does he or she feel about the relationship?

- Does the affluent client have investment advisors? How does he or she feel about these relationships?

- Does the affluent client have a financial planner? How does he or she feel about the relationship?

Process

- How many contacts are optimal for the affluent client? Investment-oriented contacts? Non-investment-oriented contacts?

- What security measures is the affluent client using to protect his or her personal and financial information?

- Who else needs to be involved in the planning process for the affluent client?

- How many face-to-face meetings would the affluent client want over the course of a year?

- Would the affluent client want a call from you about his or her personal situation when there is a sudden change in the market?

- Does the affluent client want e-mail contacts from you? What should the e-mail contacts be about?

- How often does the affluent client want an overall review of his or her financial situation and progress towards goals?

Interests

- What are the affluent client's favorite activities, TV programs, movies, and sport teams?

- Are health and fitness important to the affluent client? If so, what is his or her regimen?

- What charitable causes does the affluent client donate to? Volunteer for?

- What does the affluent client enjoy reading?

- What are the affluent client's hobbies?

- For the affluent client, what would an ideal weekend be?

- For the affluent client, what would an ideal vacation be?

As noted, these are just sample questions drawn from hundreds used by the Elite 1200 with their own affluent clients, as well as when they're profiling the affluent clients of their strategic partners. Of course, you would not use all of the questions with any particular wealthy client. What we've found is that, with practice, you'll create your own list that works best for you. Moreover, it's very likely that the list you'd use with your own wealthy clients will deviate to some degree with the list you'd use in strategic scenario sessions.

Another difference between using the Whole Client Model with the affluent directly and in *strategic scenario sessions* is the order of the questions you would ask. Specifically, it's logical to start with a wealthy client's goals and concerns when talking with him or her. However, when discussing an affluent client of a private client attorney, for instance, you might focus first on the client's level of wealth and the composition of that wealth.

A core component of this approach is to get all the information on one page. This approach proves quite powerful when you're dealing with affluent clients directly and it's been extraordinarily effective in the context of strategic scenario sessions. Doing so enables you and your strategic partner to clearly and expeditiously see the interrelationships that exist, and be better able to understand what potential products and services to recommend. The way we do this is by using a modified mind-mapping approach (Exhibit 11.1). In the center is the category Client. The other six categories are vectors off the center.

Exhibit 11.1: The Whole Client Model Graphic

Strategic scenario sessions using the Whole Client Model, when done well, tend to result in up to four or five (sometimes more) affluent clients for you to either personally meet or for whom you can provide information, analysis, or something of the sort that can potentially translate into you providing financial products or services. Hence, conducting a number of strategic scenario sessions per year with your strategic partners will fill the pipeline.

Examples of Strategic Scenario Sessions

Over three years ago, Peter arranged for two mid-sized accounting firms in his city to be licensed. For two years, he spoke with the individual accountants at these firms. He provided CPE credits to each of the firms. He even threw some of the accountants birthday parties at an upscale restaurant. And, during all this time he never saw one of their clients.

In the beginning of the third year, he adopted the approach we outlined herein. This resulted in his split with one of the accounting firms. He believed in active investment management, while the accounting firm wanted to take an indexing approach. He believed in life insurance, while this same accounting firm saw term insurance as the only viable option. It wasn't until he profiled the managing partner and the partner-in-charge of the financial services practice that he learned that they were a really bad fit for him.

In contrast, the other accounting firm was "perfect." The issues that made the other firm a non-starter were nowhere to be found. Moreover, they had business owners and high-net-worth clients that could prove extraordinarily profitable. Furthermore, in the profiling process it became clear to Peter as to what he had to do to get access to these clients. It isn't effective for him to talk to these accountants about concepts and strategies. They're much too "granular." Instead, he conducted *strategic scenario sessions* using the Whole Client Model to profile their more financially successful clients.

He used this approach with six of the partners. On average, each partner detailed four or so of his or her better clients. Of the 26 affluent accounting clients that were profiled, 21 (80.8%) became financial services clients. In total he generated $1.7 million in fees and commissions in the first year – half went to the accounting firm and half went to Peter. Additionally, the Whole Client Model unearthed additional opportunities for the accounting firm to provide its tax and reporting services.

Another financial advisor working with a private client attorney verifies the value of *strategic scenario sessions*. The two meet in the attorney's office about once every four months. On a large white board, they – using the Whole Client Model – examine five or six of the attorney's clients. This invariably leads to the financial advisor being introduced to two or three new wealthy individuals. Subsequently about 70% to 80% become clients of the financial advisor. And, those few additional wealthy clients a year have made this financial advisor a multimillionaire. Each of these clients had a net worth in excess of $50 million and all of them needed life insurance.

Strategic scenario sessions are unequivocally the most powerful way of filling the pipeline. They also are exceedingly effective in generating additional revenues for your strategic partners. For instance, the attorney from the previous example ended up billing more than $50,000 to each of his affluent clients. There were clear needs for additional legal services from each of the affluent clients profiled that only became apparent because of the Whole Client Model. So, the financial advisor as well as the attorney financially benefits and, most importantly, the wealthy clients were better served.

Non-Aligned Structured Seminars

To generate new affluent client business in concert with your strategic partners, we've found nothing is superior to *strategic scenario sessions*. Once you've reached this stage it will be quite common for you to spend a morning engaged in a *strategic scenario session* with one of your strategic partners. At the conclusion of the session, the two of you will have identified, at least, three to five excellent candidates for you to meet. Moreover, each of these prospective affluent clients will be excited to meet you because your strategic partner, in advance of the meeting, will properly prepare them.

Having said this, we've also found that many strategic partners to financial advisors are not always comfortable with the approach and want to go slower – in the beginning. This has led us to uncover a number of other approaches. One solution to this problem is conducting *non-aligned structured seminars*.

Our first intentional experience with *non-aligned structured seminars* was with a boutique tax strategy firm (our coaching client) and an international boutique investment bank. The topic was Impressionist art. The investment bank arranged for a renowned French chef and an equally renowned French pastry chef to come in from France to Greenwich, CT. The tax strategy consultancy arranged for a presentation by a leading authority on Impressionist art.

The investment bank brought nine of its clients to the seminar. Meanwhile, the tax strategy consultancy showed up with five of its clients. No client was worth less than $500 million with the aggregate wealth in the room estimated at $12 billion. During the cocktail hour, the Managing Director of the investment bank introduced their clients to the partners of the tax strategy consultancy. And, the senior partner of the consultancy introduced their clients to the relationship managers of the investment bank's private client division.

The seminar lasted two hours longer than planned as many of the wealthy clients were excited to talk about Impressionist art as well as their other personal interests and, of course, business. Within a few months, the investment bank picked up two new private clients who were initially clients of the tax strategy consultancy. Meanwhile, the consultancy picked up three assignments from the wealthy clients of the investment bank. All in all, this proved to be a very rewarding endeavor for both advisory firms.

We refer to this approach as *non-aligned structured seminars* because of the very clearly defined – often customized to the situation – implementation process involved. From whom to invite and how to invite them, to the seminar itself and the surrounding activities, to how to follow-up within what time frame, everything is prescribed in appropriate detail.

What also makes *non-aligned structured seminars* effective is that the topics are not the conventional (i.e., boring and oft times repeated) ones. We advocate you don't address such topics as asset allocation or your investment process or, for that matter, anything about you and your firm. At the same time, if your strategic partner is discussing his or her expertise, it's likely you're also not going to get the results you'd like. This focus away from the expertise of yourself and your strategic partner is why these structured seminars are "non-aligned."

We've seen financial advisors galore put on seminars that are all about them and what they're interested in. The same can be said about the other advisors they're trying to work closely with. What we're advocating is that instead of focusing the seminar on yourself or your strategic partner you keep the spotlight on the affluent clients.

What religiously works quite well, and for which there are no problems with compliance, are *non-aligned structured seminars* dealing with lifestyle issues. What we're doing is bringing your strategic partner's wealthy clients together for "insights enveloped in an experience" as opposed to an education. This proves to be a great value-add from you to your strategic partner and because we're putting on a *non-aligned structured seminar* as opposed to a talking head show, there's a subtle marketing message built into the event.

Some of the topics that have worked quite well include:

- The Essence of Luxury.

- Keeping Your Children Safe When They Go to College.

- The Art of Buying High-End Jewelry.

- The World of Fractional Jet Ownership.

- Keeping Your Secrets, Secret.

- Consigner Health Care Services.

- The Luxury Ride.

- Wines from Around the World.

- Investing in Fine Art.

- A Sneak Peak at Next Year's Fashions.

- Beyond Rolex, An Introduction to the World's Great Watch Makers.

As you can see, the topics deal with the lifestyles of the very wealthy. Experience has shown us that two areas prove to be excellent topics for the affluent – luxury and family security. Let's consider examples of how financial advisors have created *non-aligned structured seminars* with these focuses.

Luxury

For the most part, the wealthy are "into" luxury. By and large, they want a lifestyle that is replete with pleasures. You can leverage this pref-erence with well-executed *non-aligned structured seminars*.

One financial advisor conducts about four or five *non-aligned structured seminars* per year. All the topics of his seminars center on luxury for the ultra-affluent (net worth = $25 million or more). With so many such seminars, it's impossible for him to bring many of his own clients. He just doesn't have enough of them at this level of wealth. His solution was to work with an accounting firm and a law firm. Each of these strategic partners ensures that the seminar will be filled. And, all the advisors benefit by socializing with all the wealthy people in the room.

To his surprise, he's discovered that wealthy people he doesn't know, and that are not clients of either the law firm or accounting firm, have started calling him up asking for invitations to his seminars. He happily agrees to meet with them to explain to them about the seminars. A number of these over-the-transom calls have become his clients.

Family Security

Another "area" that has proven exceedingly effective is personal and family security. One of the most successful financial advisors in a wirehouse teamed up with a private client attorney who specialized in asset protection planning. However, instead of talking about financial and legal asset protection planning, they had a leading authority on personal and family security speak.

The financial advisor brought 12 high-net-worth investors to the seminar. Meanwhile, the attorney brought 14 of his clients to the seminar. Every wealthy person in the room had a minimum net worth of $10 million.

The 40-minute talk addressed a range of issues from identity theft to the dearth of security at private airports. After the presentation, the family security consultant was approached by 11 of the attendees, seven of whom were clients of the financial advisor. These seven, within a year, became clients of the attorney who set up asset protection structures for them. Of the seven, four ended up purchasing life insurance and the financial advisor executed the transactions. The financial advisor, meanwhile, cultivated two of the attorney's clients who brought in a combined $37 million in new assets.

The success of this *non-aligned structured seminar* was followed by more such seminars and more success. For the third such seminar, the attorney and financial advisor started moving downstream. They were now inviting affluent clients with about $5 million in net worth. They continued to generate business for each of them but each seminar produced more affluent clients in terms of attendees, albeit at a lower wealth level. What's important to note is that the family security consultant needed to modify his presentation to this less well-heeled audience.

Another financial advisor created a strategic partnership with a forensic accountant, and one of the initial key aspects of their partnership was the *non-aligned structured seminar* they held for divorce attorneys. They brought in a family security consultant to address how to legally and effectively obtain a great deal of information, often incriminating information, on wayward affluent spouses. What proved to be very effective in this seminar were the handout materials including a bound set of guidelines explaining how to collect the non-financial information (keeping in mind that the financial autopsy is conducted by the forensic accountant).

The forensic accountant filled the seminar with the appropriate divorce attorneys – both current referral sources and prospects. The financial advisor contributed the family security consultant. The result was business for everyone.

The forensic accountant obtained more situations to work on, the family security consultant also generated business, and the financial advisor started getting wealthy – almost all female – divorcées as clients. For the financial advisor, these were "perfect" clients. There weren't any other financial advisors involved with these affluent individuals, and they turned to him to address all their investment and estate planning needs. What was so nice for the financial advisor is that he was referred affluent clients before leaving the seminar, and he ended up establishing professional relationships with the divorce attorneys such that two of them became clients in only a few weeks of the seminar.

Another financial advisor constructed a *non-aligned structured seminar* in conjunction with a property and casualty brokerage firm and a trusts and estate attorney with a solid reputation among leading art dealers. She brought in the family security consultant and the art dealer, as well as the attorney, delivered affluent art aficionados to a number of seminars they held on the topic of protecting the art from thieves. No more than 20 wealthy people were in attendance at any one seminar.

The family security consultant showed the audience how easy it is conceptually to steal paintings out of houses that supposedly have the finest security systems around. He also – sponsored by the financial advisor and the property & casualty brokerage firm – would arrange to "ghost" any of the houses of the wealthy people in the audience. This means, that the family security consultant will, with the permission of the owner, break into the owner's house and "steal" a painting thereby showing the weaknesses in the owner's security system and, more importantly, how they can be secured.

On average, about 20% of the attendees took the family security consultant up on the offer. And, nearly all the houses of these wealthy individuals were successfully compromised. This usually resulted in re-evaluating and increasing the insurance on the paintings as well as other property insurance. It also translated into clients for the financial advisor, which was a product of the recommendations of both the property & casualty agents as well as the family security consultant.

The use of the family security consultant to attract the affluent not only has been proven highly effective with private client attorneys but has also been very effective when financial advisors have teamed up with property and casualty brokers, art dealers, accountants, real estate brokers, high-end jewelers, divorce attorneys, appraisers, and corporate attorneys. We've found that working with a family security consultant that is truly expert in working with private clients, able to present well, and is capable of modifying his or her presentation opens the doors to a panoply of other types of advisors to the affluent.

With each of these *non-aligned structured seminars*, you and your strategic partner can design them so that they can – in an often-unobtrusive manner – lead back to products and services the two of you can provide. Even in those instances when the road back is too erratic, your strategic partner is building stronger relationships with his or her affluent clients. Meanwhile, you're getting the opportunity to meet a number of wealthy potential clients in a very positive context.

Non-aligned structured seminars such as these, while quite powerful in generating new business for all involved, must be managed extremely well for them to work. There are many ways these events can get derailed and you have to make sure they stay on track. However, the rewards of conducting *non-aligned structured seminars* can be tremendous.

Three Play

With respect to *non-aligned structured seminars,* the examples we've been considering are between a financial advisor and his or her strategic partner. In taking the concept of *non-aligned structured seminars* to the next level, a financial advisor teams up with two non-competing strategic partners. The two areas that we've often employed – luxury and family security – work well with seminars involving two strategic partners.

A life insurance agent (who only sold life insurance) arranged for a hedge fund (money management) and a private bank (which only provided lending and transaction services) to invite some of their more affluent clients to an introduction of the latest personal technologies coupled with a scotch tasting. The hedge fund and the bank, in total, delivered 27 affluent clients (average net worth was $15 million). The life insurance agent arranged for the latest in high-tech "toys" as well as the scotch.

Referrals from these two strategic partners resulted in life insurance sales of more than $3 million in first year commissions over a two-year time period. The hedge fund, as well as the private bank, reported that they found the experience very rewarding.

One financial advisor found success in having a family security consultant address the benefits of a crisis intervention plan. In a study of 427 wealthy individuals, only 16.6% of them even had crisis intervention plans in place (Exhibit 11.2).

Exhibit 11.2: Currently Have a Crisis Intervention Plan

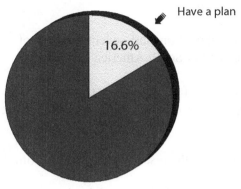

N = 427 wealthy individuals

Source: Safe & Sound (National Underwriter, 2004).

What proves to be especially interesting to the affluent is the part of the presentation that deals with the "limits of crisis intervention process." Just consider:

- The yacht hijacked by modern day pirates in the Caribbean. The family kept on board and held for ransom. All the while the people were assaulted.

- The mistaken kidnapping of the daughter of a very prominent and exceptionally wealthy family who was sold into white slavery and transported to the Far East. (We say "mistaken" because if the slavers knew of her pedigree, they would not have targeted her. Unfortunately, at the time, she was rebelling against her family and "hanging out" with a "fast crowd.")

- The private jet that was repeatedly vandalized. And, on one such occasion, a 12 year old member of the ultra-affluent family that owned the jet was unlucky to be there when the vandals appeared and crippled him.

- The daughter of a celebrity on the rebound from a particularly bad divorce was "set up" by a potentially very violent professional criminal. He had provided her with a considerable amount of drugs and had her star in a particularly explicit pornographic movie that was sent to the celebrity. The motivation was extortion.

- The abduction and severe beating of a business owner kidnapped in South America.

The job of the family security consultant is to resolve the crisis and provide appropriate ongoing support. With respect to the above situations:

- Facilitate the rescue of the family from the yacht.

- Arrange for the return of the daughter sold into white slavery.

- Ensure that the family's private jet is secure and the family kept safe.

- Make sure the celebrity's daughter is safe and assist the legal team involved in the case.

- Arrange for the return of the business owner kidnapped in South America.

In situations like these, the wealthy first and foremost want the crisis contained and resolved. Not surprisingly, and what is often justifiable, the wealthy want their "pound of flesh." In extreme situations like these, the financial elite want revenge. They want to make the criminals who hurt them and their loved ones so badly pay.

The job of the family security consultant is to resolve the crisis and provide appropriate ongoing support. This can very well mean coordinating a team of specially trained rescue operatives to board a yacht and forcibly take command in order to rescue the family from pirates. If in the process, the criminals are hurt, so be it. However, the goal is not to hurt criminals but to rescue the family, and the less conflict the better.

Returning to our three play: the financial advisor delivered the family security consultant. A boutique law firm with transnational private clients provided seven of them (minimum net worth = $50 million). Six more affluent clients of similar wealth were provided by an accounting firm with an international tax practice. All the affluent attendees owned their own yachts as well as their own jets. They and their families traveled the world.

The presentation on crisis intervention struck a chord, especially since none of the affluent had taken any preparatory steps to date. Aside from the family security consultant, the accounting firm, the law firm, and the financial advisors all obtained new or additional business from the wealthy attendees.

The Need for Choreography

It's not enough for you to bring in an authority on a luxury topic or a family security consultant or some other authority to address a non-financial topic of considerable interest to the affluent. It's not enough for you to bring these experts into a room of interested wealthy people provided by strategic partners. You must do these things, and you must orchestrate every aspect of the seminar to maximize your relationships with the potential wealthy clients in attendance.

What we've seen is that those financial advisors who fail to carefully manage the entire process from how to invite the wealthy to how to follow-up with them, more often than not, fail to generate new affluent clients. More upsetting is that failing to astutely manage the *non-aligned structured seminar* from beginning to end can prove deleterious with respect to all in attendance – the wealthy, your strategic partner, and the expert you brought in. And, the stakes are often too high to have this happen.

At the same time, you need to ensure that:

- Your strategic partner (or two) who are filling the room, or helping to do so, are very satisfied with the results they're getting. This generally means more business for them.

- The authority you are using to attract and educate and engage the affluent audience is very satisfied. As with your strategic partners, this generally means more business for him or her.

- Lastly, you need the seminar to result in more business for you.

To make all this work well requires that the *non-aligned structured seminar*, from beginning to end, be well choreographed. Having a meeting for the sake of getting all these people in the same room can prove wasteful or even disadvantageous unless you take the time and effort to structure the seminar (hence the name) so that it results in the optimal desired outcomes for all involved. In the hands of experienced professionals, this is far from difficult. However, unless you or your team is adept at putting such a project together, it's advisable to bring in the appropriate professionals.

Conclusions

Once you have a strategic partnership with an accountant, a private client attorney, or some other non-competing professional, you still have to fill the pipeline with many, many potential affluent clients. Herein, we discussed two proven approaches to filling the pipeline – *strategic scenario sessions* and *non-aligned structured seminars*.

Of course, *strategic scenario sessions* and *non-aligned structured seminars* are not exclusive. In coaching financial advisors on filling the pipeline, we regularly combine the two approaches. As noted, *non-aligned structured seminars*, for many strategic partners of financial advisors, is value-added in it's own right and has enabled us to then move to *strategic scenario sessions*. At the same time, well-executed *strategic scenario sessions* are also value-added by creating business opportunities for your strategic partner.